THE LIFE AND TIMES OF BOB CRATCHIT

DIXIE DISTLER

DEDICATION

I dedicate this book to all the silent and unsung heroes who selflessly help a fellow traveler in need; whose good deeds will forever ripple through time and space.

DIXIE DISTLER

ACKNOWLEDGMENTS

I am grateful for the editorial assistance of Willy Mathes.
www.bookeditorcoach.com

I also thank my husband, family, and friends who encouraged me
to keep writing so Bob Cratchit's story could finally be told.

Most importantly, I acknowledge Mr. Charles Dickens, who
brought us *A Christmas Carol* through his mastery of storytelling.
His timeless classic has set the Christmas tone for generations.
I am humbled to expand on his masterpiece with
The Life and Times of Bob Cratchit.

Marley was *alive*, to begin with …

Chapter 1

The ripples you create return to you in waves. That's what Father used to say, at least, Robert Cratchit thought, wondering deep in his heart what it would take for him to right the wrong he'd done to Mr. Ebenezer Scrooge.

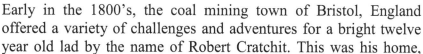

Early in the 1800's, the coal mining town of Bristol, England offered a variety of challenges and adventures for a bright twelve year old lad by the name of Robert Cratchit. This was his home, the place of his birth and youth, and he genuinely loved every aspect of this active, budding city.

To the west were the busy ports, running off the river Avon, where he and his friends could watch as a variety of ships would carefully maneuver the cluttered harbor before safely docking. Robert's mother, Rebecca, (or Becky, as she liked to be called) firmly forbade her young son from being anywhere near the vicinity of the docks, fearing perilous consequences for him if he fell victim to the *bad element* that lurked there. Nevertheless, the boys continued to scamper down to the wharf, particularly near the warehouses where the ships were being built. Here, they would watch in awe as the recently constructed crafts were released into the murky waters of the "Floating Harbor" to embark upon their maiden voyages.

On such a day, Robert and two of his friends revisited their favorite spot on the boardwalk; a weathered, descending walkway near the pier where the young lads had a clear view of the ships and waterfront below. The typically vacated pier was crowded with people waiting for the exciting ceremony involved with a ship launching.

Next to the boys, a young woman was looking toward the deep channel as a Schooner sailed slowly past, headed for open waters. Near the bow, a tall slender man waved and, with a girlish giggle, the woman waved eagerly in return. "Do you know him?" Robert asked drumming up polite conversation.

"Aye, that's my husband. He's first mate to Captain York. They're sailing the Constantine to the colonies in America," the woman responded.

Looking closer, Robert saw a smaller boy standing next to the first mate on the ship. Instinctively, he waved to the young boy who began waving in return. "Is that your son next to him?"

"Ney lad, that's just a cabin boy. I pray they fair well on this voyage. My husband was shaken by this passage. He rarely attempts a crossing in the heat of summer. Bad storms abound when the sun is at its peak."

"Good day to you, young sir," the woman nodded courteously to Robert and hurried down the boardwalk to keep pace with the Constantine. Robert returned his attention to that of the crowd as the newly built ship was preparing to touch water.

"Did you see that boy on the Constantine?" Robert asked his friends. "He's no older than us, and now he's off on a great adventure at sea while we're stuck here on land! Someday I'm going to sail away just like him, and have my own adventures to tell."

"We should all go together," Randall added. "That way, if we run into pirates, we could fight as a team."

"Hey, I think they're getting ready to launch her," mumbled Robert, squinting as he shifted slightly to the left, hoping it would give him a better view from his perch, "Look, Wayne. What's the name on her?"

"Don't know," whispered Wayne, leaning slightly forward and straining to see around the large man standing in front of him. "What d'ya think, Randall?"

Sharply, Wayne poked his friend with his elbow and pointed toward a large ship that was surrounded on each side by a troop of sweat soaked, brawny men who were tightly gripping bulky ropes that were woven through a series of pulleys attached to the deck of the massive vessel. With great care, the men strained and wrestled with the awkward tethers as they controlled the ships sluggish decent toward its watery destination.

"Stop it," Randall growled, "I see it. But I can't make out the name either."

For a brief moment, the three young boys stared silently at the great ship, each one caught up in their own idea of what they would have christened the vessel.

The Penny, that's what I'd call her, Wayne imagined, nodding slightly. *If the name's good enough for my little dog, it is good enough for a ship.*

I'd name it after my mum's favorite flower, reflected Randall in his silence. *The Rose. Yes, the Rose. That's what she'd be called.*

The Polly, that's what I would have named her, thought Robert. *It's a pretty name for such a good looking vessel.*

"That ship be the Claria, lads."

Unexpectedly stirred from their daydreaming, the boys flinched when they heard the low, raspy voice speak from behind them. With guarded care, they spun around and saw a scruffy old seaman staring down at them. The deep creases on his bristly weather-beaten face were partially concealed under his grubby captain's hat, and his tattered old coat reeked of rotten fish and musty pipe smoke.

"Aye, she's a fully rigged ship, that one" he croaked out, shifting slightly on his feet and flashing them a toothless grin, "She be mak'in her maiden voyage to the West Indies or such, less'n she meets with a big storm along the way an' she be smashed to wee bits on the rocks."

The old seaman let out an unsettling low, throaty cackle and shuffled toward the boys.

All at once, the three young lads gasped and, after almost falling over each other, stumbled clumsily to their feet and ran like scared rabbits toward their homes. Slightly winded as he dashed through the city streets, Robert thought about the crazy old seafarer and the warnings from his mother about the dangers at the harbor.

That was close. Mother was right. There are some peculiar individuals at the docks. It looks like we're going to have to find us a new favorite spot for watching ships.

To the north of the city were the local coalmines. More notably, the Kingswood pits where Robert's father, Peter, labored as a collier in the bowels of the earth, missing any chance to see daylight six of the seven days of the week. In the mines, where he worked alongside men and boys, there were treacherous and unsanitary conditions, which were evident by the unbearable, stifling heat, stagnant air, pools of filthy water and the genuine threat of flash floods and cave-ins.

Robert eagerly looked forward to the days when he, his older sister Elizabeth (who preferred Lizzy) and his mother would surprise his father by meeting him at day's end, near the entrance of the mines and escort him home.

After a grueling day in the mine, the sight of his family waiting patiently by the foreman's building and their eager conversation about the events of the day eased the weariness Peter felt in his tired, aching body.

"Here you go my boy." Peter plopped his dusty black cap on top of Roberts head and watched as the oversized rim slid down over the boys face, covering his eyes. The miner grinned at this amusing sight and his teeth seemed to glow a bright white in contrast to his sooty, blackened face.

With a sheepish grin, Robert readjusted the hat above his brow, "See Father, it almost fits. Soon I'll be a miner, too!"

"We'll see about that, lad," Peter replied as he rested his strong, calloused hand on his son's small shoulder, "We'll see".

Peter was a third generation coal miner. Admiring his father as he did, Robert fully expected to be the fourth; that is, unless his mother and father had their way. Both parents were well aware of the perils of the mines and the dead-end, lifelong commitment of this profession and they desired a better future for their son.

Becky intended to leverage her education to broaden the opportunities for both her children. She was raised and educated in a relatively well-to-do London home. At the exclusive girl's school she attended, the young socialite was every bit the envy of her classmates. Her father, a coal distributor, had little time for his children and her mother utilized most of her time in social circles; so much of Becky's childhood was structured by her nannies.

Thus, it was only natural that Becky passed her learned skills to her children at home, working with each of them on their studies after they returned from school. Peter was pleased, knowing his wife was preparing their children for a better life than that of a miner's family. During most days, after chores were finished, math problems were practiced on slate with chalk. When available, blood stained butcher paper was used for practicing their penmanship, often until the quill no longer held ink. In the evening, Robert and Lizzy read aloud from the family bible to their parents by candle light.

But Robert's days were not entirely consumed by school work and chores. The scrappy young lad often played hard with the other boys in the village. Although somewhat perilous, the streets of Bristol served well as a playground for the youth of the city. The curls in the young Cratchit's longish, sandy colored hair often hid his brown eyes during a fast-paced game of stickball or tag. Occasionally, he even tied his hair back into a pony tail, which was his mother's cue to cut his locks. And cutting young Robert's cherished mane was never an easy task.

"Stop fidgeting, Robert," growled Becky, as she attempted to snip a lock of hair with her kitchen shears, "I'd rather cut the hair and not the boy, if you please."

"Why must I always get my hair trimmed? It was just starting to grow out," protested the young Cratchit as he shifted again on the chair.

Robert winced as his mother clipped another cluster of hair, "My dear son," Becky responded, letting the small clump drift to the floor," Yesterday your *ponytail* came undone while you were playing games with your friends, obscuring your view, whereby you tripped over Wayne's dog, Penny."

"I didn't hurt her," retorted Robert in his defense.

Becky moved to the back of his head and lifted up another bunch of hair. "True, Penny was not harmed, but you fell into old Miss Adorel's flower cart, knocking it over." This time Robert groaned and rolled his eyes when he heard the scissors clip the remainder of his ponytail.

"And then you tumbled into the gutter, skinning your arm and leg quite severely," she continued as she dropped the bundle of hair to the floor, "and that is why you need your hair trimmed, my dear boy. Besides, I believe you look better with it shorter."

"Well, Wayne and Randall say I look more mature with my hair longer," he responded with a slight smirk, "and Randall's older sister, Polly, says it makes me look handsome."

Robert's eyes widened when he realized what he had just said.

"Ah, so little Polly says it makes you look handsome," Becky snickered as she cut another thick clump of hair from his head and let it fall to the floor.

With an unpleasant expression on his face, Robert blew out a low "Hmpft" and slumped lower in the chair with his arms folded across his chest. By no surprise to Becky, there was not another word spoken during the remainder of the haircutting session.

Aside from Robert's occasional cockiness, surfacing from a lack of experience and maturity, the most striking features of the young Cratchit were his thirst for knowledge—a keen listener when adults were speaking, he would also regularly ask thoughtful questions—and his obvious compassion for friends, family and creatures alike.

Sunday was the Cratchit's *family day,* and the one day of the week when they could all be together, far away from the pressures of work and city life. On one of these typical Sunday afternoons, as Robert and his family followed the familiar pathway to their favorite spot, he noticed how the brisk autumn air carried the woodsy scent of the changing season through the forest. All around him the towering trees were beginning to bear fall colors, with their leaves displaying brilliant shades of browns, reds and rich yellows.

"We're here!" sang out Lizzy as she took Becky's hand and led her to a shady location under an old, twisted oak tree.

Becky gently pushed back the curly brown locks from her daughter's forehead and smiled, "You never forget, do you?"

Giggling, Lizzy took the knitting basket from her mother, "How could I forget, it's so beautiful and peaceful here."

"Give me a hand, Robert, my boy," called Peter as he carried a large quilt over to the old oak and started to unfold it, "then we'll be off."

After Robert and his father spread the quilt, Lizzy snuck up behind Robert and tapped him on the shoulder with a quick "You're it!" before running for the other side of the tree as her brother chased close behind.

Peter and Becky watched their children play in the meadow as Becky let out a sigh, "I hope that girl does not tear her dress. She's still wearing her church dress and decides to play tag. I suppose I should find my blue thread and plan to be up late mending tonight."

Peter laughed at his wife's frustration as he watched his children play. Every day Lizzy looked more and more like her mother with her long dark hair, wearing her favorite blue dress that seemed to fit most occasions.

After the children tired of running, Becky and Lizzy settled beneath the aged tree with their knitting while father and son gathered their cane poles, fishing pail, and bait before cutting across an overgrown meadow, toward the pond.

Robert loved to go fishing at the local pond with his father. He especially looked forward to when their lines were in the water, a few quiet minutes had passed between them, and their time of talking together would begin.

"Watch the ripples in the water, as I throw this stone," Peter instructed Robert. "Do you see how the ripples run along the top of the water in every direction?"

"Yes, Father," Robert replied, as he watched the small waves.

"You are the stone," Peter continued. "The water is mankind, and the ripples are your deeds. The stone landing in the water is you among your fellow man. Everything you do and say, whether good or bad, ripples across mankind in all directions. This is why your deeds must be good, so your ripples are good as well. On the contrary, the ripples of a bad act will hurt people. Do you understand what I'm telling you, Robert?"

"Yes Father, I think I do. If I lie, cheat, or steal, I hurt more than just the person who I've wronged. The world is a lesser place because of the lying, cheating or stealing. But if I help someone in need, I help more than just that one person. My good deed makes the world a better place for all."

Peter looked away from Robert, and began staring at the water, nodding his head. "Humph, good lad," he said, holding back his pride in his young son's comprehension.

After awhile, Peter told Robert to fetch water in the empty fishing pail that rested behind them. Robert did as his father asked and set it, mostly full, between them.

"Now, pick up a small pebble, drop it in the middle of the pail and tell me what you see in the ripples."

Robert continued with his life lesson, by dropping a small stone into the bucket, curious as to what his father wanted him to learn. "Father!" Robert exclaimed in fascination. "The ripples went out from the stone and then bounced off the sides of the pail and returned to the middle, where I first dropped the stone."

"You tell me what you see. Now, tell me what it *means*."

Robert thought for only a moment before explaining in an excited voice, "The ripples from me, both good and bad, indeed spread out—but eventually my deeds come back on me. If I do good things, then good things will come back to me—but if I do bad, then bad things will happen to me, as well!"

Peter put his arm around his son's shoulders and smiled. "That's right, my boy. You know, you seem to understand more about life than most men I know. And, Robert, this is why we're here beside this pond, discussing such things. I believe it's our purpose in life to spread good ripples among those around us wherever we go." Picking up a pebble himself and throwing it out into the pond, he said, "At the end of a man's life, he will be judged, *not* by his wealth or social standing, but by the *ripples* he leaves behind."

Chapter 2

It was a cool fall day when Peter was more than fifty meters below the earth's surface, shoveling coal into a trolley cart next to three other men, who were swinging their pick axes against the coal rich wall before them. Peter was the first to feel a vibration beneath his feet. Resting the blade of his shovel on the ground, he briefly paused and listened. "Hold up!" he called to the ax men. Curious about his signal to suspend their sweaty labor, each man stopped and stood upright, staring blankly at Peter. At the first sign of coal dust falling from the ceiling, dimly lit by a hanging lantern, Peter sprang into action.

"Move, by God, move!" he cried out, grabbing each man by the arm and flinging them past himself toward the cave's entrance. The third man barely cleared the area, before the main ceiling beam gave way and crashed to the cave floor. The avalanche of coal and rock forced Peter face down to the ground and pushed the crusty air from his lungs. With the wind knocked out of him, his eyes closed in the darkness as coal dust swirled throughout the tomb-like enclosure in which he was now trapped. Several fallen wooden beams, however, had lodged against each other, and now served as a shelter for his body, holding back the earth from above. Separated from the survivors, unable to push against the beams on his back, Peter laid perfectly still, incapable of drawing in even one last breath of air.

Darkness gave way to light, as Peter stood in the doorway of his small, company owned flat, watching his wife read a lesson to their two children, all seated at the small table in their kitchen. His ghostly presence felt dreamlike as he struggled to pull air into his lungs to call out his wife's name.

Becky stopped mid-sentence, turned toward Peter, as did Robert and Lizzy, all looking at him without seeing him. Becky broke the silence with a sound of dread in her voice, "I just felt a cold chill on my back."

Peter's left hand was the only sign of human existence the three men found, as they returned to the cave-in site through the thick coal dust. "He's alive!" one man exclaimed, as he grasped Peter's left hand and felt it squeeze his own. Frantically, the men pushed the loose stone away, clearing an air passage to his mouth. A moment later, they heard a low, raspy gasp come from their fallen co-worker. Without words, they continued quickly dragging stone after stone off of him, until finally, Peter's body could be yanked out of the rubble completely. "Careful, mates," one miner cautioned. "Poor chap has lost his right arm. It's cut clean off!"

With nothing more than a single lantern to see by, one man pulled Peter's blood soaked sleeve off of his shirt to reveal the arm that now ended at the elbow. Blood hemorrhaged from the open wound with each beat of his heart. He then took the sleeve and tied it around the unconscious man's upper arm as tightly as he could to slow the bleeding.

The other two men carried him up and out of the shaft and laid him on a horse-drawn wagon, which rushed him to the company infirmary for care.

For days, Becky sat by her husband's bedside. Peter was ghostly pale having lost so much blood, yet he clung to life with each labored breath that pushed against three broken ribs. "Wake up my love. Drink this." Becky repeated her encouraging phrase time and time again as she raised her husband's head to the spoon of broth.

The company doctor approached and stood at the foot of the bed and told Becky, "If he lives, I'll cut the rest of the arm off. What's there is badly damaged and prone to infection. Besides, it would just be in the way if we left it hanging there."

As the doctor walked away without so much as a response from Becky who was dwelling on the Doctor's use of the word "*if*", Peter moved his head and moaned for the first time. Sure that her husband had heard the doctor, she began talking to him constantly, looking for a sign, any sign, that he was hearing and understanding her.

"Do you remember when we first met, Peter?" Trying to stir a response from her husband, she found herself reminiscing for her own comfort as well. "I rode with my father from London to Bristol on a coal run so he could buy a wagon load of coal for his company. He left me with the horses while he went inside to pay for the load and you shoveled the coal into the wagon. Ah, you were such a handsome devil, I confess I forgot my situation and couldn't turn my eyes away from you. Do you remember how embarrassed I was when you caught me staring at you, Peter?"

Peter continued to breathe rhythmically after instinctively swallowing the next spoon of broth from the woman who now saw the seventeen year old boy from years before. "Oh my father was furious with me when I told him that you and I had talked up a storm and that I wanted to see you again, while we were riding back to London." Lowering the tone of her voice to mimic her father, Becky re-enacted the lecture she heard that day, "Not in my lifetime will any daughter of mine relate to a coal miner! It is just not proper for a polished lady to socialize with anyone from his class. We will never speak of this again and you, my dear child, will never again travel with me to Bristol!"

"Well," Becky continued as though she was telling her story to Peter for the first time, "you just don't tell a stubborn London lass what she cannot do, unless you want her to do it. So two weeks later, there I was, riding on a coal cart with my father's foreman back to Bristol after swearing him to silence, at least as far as my father was concerned. And there you were, more striking than I remembered. No question about it. If I wasn't before, I was certain now that I was in love with a sweaty, filthy, coal miner who spoke to me so tenderly."

Combing her fingers through her husband's hair still matted with coal dust, she reassured him with the words he wanted to hear every time he reminded her what she gave up when she left London for the last time, disinherited and alone, "And I tell you my love, the day we eloped and started our lives together was the happiest day of my life. If I had it to do all over again, the only thing I would change would be to marry you a day sooner."

"I love hearing that story."

Becky turned quickly to see her fourteen year old daughter Lizzy standing at the foot of the bed, watching intently as her mother coaxed her father to cling to this world. "I didn't see you, my dear. Where is your brother?"

"He left a few hours ago to play with his friends Wayne and Randall. I don't understand him, mother. He acts as though nothing is wrong; as though none of this is real."

Becky shook her head and replied, "Don't you worry my love. He is very close to his father, yet cannot accept the changes that now confront us. When the mine collapsed, all of our lives changed forever. Robert is not ready to accept our new lives. We will do what we can for your father today, and give your brother the time he needs to face tomorrow."

"I suppose you're right," sighed Lizzy as she tenderly took the bowl from her mother.

"Let me sit with him for a while. You should get some rest."

Becky wiped the tears from her eyes and agreed, "Perhaps you're right. Keep giving him as much broth as he can take, and keep talking to him. I have seen him move a couple of times as I talk, so I know for certain he hears us."

With that said, Becky stood and leaned over to kiss her husband on the lips before giving her seat, to Lizzy. Walking away, she did not see Peter lick his wife's kiss from his lips, which nourished his spirit just as her broth had nourished his body.

Lizzy sat quietly, studying the features of the man who had always been her pillar of strength. As instructed, she managed to get her father to swallow a couple of spoons of broth, but the thought of a one-sided conversation seemed awkward.

"Father?"

Maybe it was the idea of asking questions to which she would receive no answer. Maybe she was just so accustomed to receiving her father's attention when they talked that she missed looking at his brown eyes that would squint when he smiled at his little girl.

After a few more uncomfortable moments of silence, Lizzy found her voice, "Let me make sure I understand. I can ask you or tell you anything I like and you can't disagree? I think I may like this." Lizzy giggled nervously as she patted her hands on her father's chest.

"Alright then, let me ask you something. Why did you say no to Andrew Taylor the other day when he asked you if he could court me? I've known him my whole life and we are best friends. Besides, Mother was just two years older than me when she first met you, right? I just stood right here and heard her telling you about the way she fell in love with you, so why can't a boy court me? Did you ever stop to consider that I may be in love with him?"

Peter lay emotionless as his little girl tried to convince him that she is more an adult than he realized.

"Is it that you think I am too young? Or maybe you think Andrew isn't right for me? After all, he is the toughest boy at school. He wins every fight he is in. Is that it? You don't like the way he is always getting into fights? Don't you think I should have a husband who can protect me?"

Thinking more about her questions and the way she realized that Andrew indeed seemed to get involved in a lot of fist fights, she thought more about her feelings for him.

"He does seem to have a bad temper. I even saw him push his own sister into a mud puddle the other day and just stand there to laugh at her. Father—I don't think Andrew is the right boy for me." Before touching the spoon filled with broth to his lips, Lizzy watched as the corners her father's lips moved to form a slight smile.

A couple of hours passed as Lizzy realized more and more how important her father was to her life and their family. After moments of silent reflection, Lizzy spoke to her father's very soul, "Father, the greatest gift you have ever given me is your love for my mother."

Suddenly, as she was distracted by a loud thud to her right, Lizzy gazed over and watched as her young brother passed cautiously through the large wooden and glass door leading into the infirmary.

"Mother wants you to come home for dinner," Robert informed his sister. "I'll stay with Father for a while."

"Are you alright, Robert?"

"No, this isn't fair," Robert replied, relieved that someone finally asked how *he* was feeling. "Why did he have to stay behind to save those other men? From what I hear, he was the closest one to the entrance, yet he stayed to get the other men out first. He wasn't thinking about us, he was only thinking about them!"

As Robert's tears began to fall, Lizzy looked at their father; motionless except for his slow rhythmic breathing, before turning back to her younger brother, "You're wrong, Robert. He was thinking of us as well as the families of each of those men. Had he turned to run from the mine, leaving the others behind, he would have died inside. For the rest of his life he would have been haunted by the deaths of the men he could have saved."

Robert wiped his tears and looked at the man who clung to life.

"Look at him, Robert," Lizzy continued. "Would you rather have a father who is whole on the inside and broken on the outside, or complete in body yet hollow within? Don't you see? He could no more have turned his back on those men than you could fly like a bird."

Lizzy explained to her younger brother, as their mother did for her, the need for him to keep feeding and talking to their father. "He hears us Robert. I know he does. Just tell him how much we need him and how much we love him."

With a nod and a slight smile, Robert's sister handed him the bowl and left the room.

Robert sat silently on the left side of his father's bed. Staring across Peter's chest, he fixated on the bindings wrapped tightly around his father's short arm, noting that at the injured end the bandage was red from the blood that continued to seep from his severed limb.

"Young fellow? How's your father?" he heard as the doctor approached the other side of the bed.

"Doing better, sir," Robert replied more as a wishful thought than a diagnosis.

The doctor proceeded to unwrap the long bloodstained pieces of white cloth, removing the old bandage to replace it with a new one, whistling as he inspected the wound for signs of infection. For Robert, the sight of the missing limb with black thread sewn through the loose skin was horrifying. The remainder of the limb didn't even resemble the muscular arm that used to lift him and his sister with ease.

"Keep giving him that broth lad," the doctor said as he walked across the room to another unconscious man who rested alone.

Robert got two spoons of broth past his father's lips before spilling the third. Disgusted with himself, but more so, the sudden and dramatic change to his life, he stood and walked to the window, wishing to see anything other than his father in this condition.

Between the buildings across the road, he saw a sliver of the meadow that led to the path he walked so many times with his father. The path that led from the Kingswood pits where his father mined to their home on the second floor of the flats owned by the mining company. Beyond their home was the path to the woods where he played; and the pond where he fished so often with his father.

Robert shook loose the daydream and looked behind himself to the bed where his father laid unconscious, wondering if there would ever be another day when the two would fish together. Determined now to make it so, he returned to his seat by the bed and lifted the spoon of broth to his father's lips.

"Father? Do you remember our fishing trip last Sunday? Do you remember our walk home when I asked you if we could go fishing again, and you promised me we would? Well sir, I'm here to tell you that you are going to keep your promise."

Spoon after spoon, Robert continued until the bowl was empty. "All gone! Good, Father. Now you can rest." While holding Peter's hand between both of his own, Robert closed his eyes and imagined himself fishing next to his father. Robert smiled as he realized that he would be baiting his father's hook from now on, instead of his father baiting his as he had done in the past.

Slowly, but deliberately, he felt a squeeze on his hand. Opening his eyes, he looked at the man's large hand as the fingers wrapped around his. Excited by the movement, Robert was speechless for a moment as he looked back to the eyes that were now barely open, looking into his.

Three weeks after regaining consciousness and much of his strength while recuperating at home, Peter told Becky that he was going to walk back to the infirmary to let the doctor check his arm.

"I'll walk with you," Becky instantly offered.

"No!" Peter sharply responded. Realizing Becky didn't deserve such a brash reply, he softened his voice to explain, "I'm sorry love, but I have to go alone. I won't be home tonight, but you can come see me in the infirmary tomorrow."

Becky looked in her husband's eyes and saw a sense of fear that she had never seen in him before. More than anything, she wanted to be there to hold him, but she knew her husband. She knew he would not want her to see him crying out in agony as the doctor sawed through the remainder of his limb.

Chapter 3

Since Peter had, indeed, lost his right arm in the mining accident, he was soon dismissed from the company. "I have no need for a one-armed digger," his foreman callously informed him.

The small, three-room flat the Cratchits had occupied was company owned, so being dismissed from the company meant they were evicted from their home, as well. Within days, the discomfited family of four literally carried their few personal belongings to London where they slept in shelters at night and looked for work by day. Becky found work as a laundress, earning a shilling a day—barely enough to feed the family one meager meal each night. The work was exhausting, as she moved large bundles through a series of washing vats and scrubbing tubs, in addition to mending rips and holes in garments and sheets. At night, her hands would crack and bleed from the constant exposure to lye she received, as she pulled the wet fabrics from the heated vats.

Being a burly fellow, Peter—even without a right arm—could complete an honest day's work. He cleaned stables and cared for horses at the local blacksmith's. With his and his wife's diligent efforts, they soon saved enough money to pay the first month's rent for a dismal two-room basement flat. By the end of their first day there, however, the Cratchit family realized it was a place more suited for the rats than any human occupant.

Peter despised the city, but for Robert, it was an adventure for all of his senses. Out on the streets, there were perpetual crowds of people, always on the move, seemingly with nowhere to go, but always in a hurry to get there. The elite and wealthy coexisted with those of want and hunger, yet paid them no never-mind. In one area, streets were swept clean and walls of buildings were scrubbed; while a block away, filth provided a refuge to sewer rats and alley cats.

The smells of the city were even more of a contrast than the sights and sounds. Those who could afford to do so lived in polished burrows; but for most, open sewers carried fetid waste water to underground aqueducts designed and built by the Roman Empire centuries earlier. The stench from these sewers was beyond offensive. Potable water was brought into London from the river Thames, but it did little to remove the acrid odor on any given hot summer day. Beyond the problem of water, reeking garbage accumulated in alleys, until the horse drawn carts carried it out of sight.

The one constant for every dwelling, rich or poor, was the soot from the thousands of coal burning fires across the city. Even in the heat of the summer, coal was burned for cooking and heating water. The horizon loomed like an open canvas of black plumes, rising from chimneys, just to settle in a thick blanket of black dust on roof and road alike. Without rain to cleanse the mortar and brick, the city would be buried in its own ash.

The Cratchit's small basement dwelling itself stank of poverty. The stone walls were perpetually damp, which fueled the musty smell that lingered inside. Their clothes shared the same smells of mold and mildew, no matter how fervently Becky scrubbed them on the wash board. Peter and Becky slept in the second room on a straw stuffed mattress, while Robert and Lizzy unrolled their mats on opposite sides of the first room to sleep.

Each night, Robert curled up under the one window that was at ground level, listening to the infrequent wagons and pedestrians on the cobblestone street, until the dreams of his night's sleep took him back to the fresh air and fields of green near his childhood home. And each morning, all four Cratchits would awaken to the clamorous noise arising from throngs of people going about their business on the street above them.

The landlord who owned the building—and several more like it—was the company of Scrooge and Marley. Peter learned early on that going to the office of Scrooge and Marley to do anything other than pay the rent was futile. Once, he asked if the water leaks that trickled through the stone walls during a heavy rain and covered the floor in the flat could be fixed; to which, Mr. Ebenezer Scrooge snapped back, "If you don't like your accommodations, sir, then leave them for your room in the King's Palace!" Walking out, after humbly apologizing to Mr. Scrooge for the interruption, he could hear both men snickering behind their desks, as Mr. Scrooge shuffled a fist full of coins, just to enjoy the sound of money.

Some days, Robert met his father at the stables and helped as much as he could. He was never allowed in the mines as a young lad, but here at the stables he could be with his father, even when there was work to be done. Peter enjoyed Robert's companionship, as well, never missing an opportunity to share with him whatever 'words of wisdom' that might arise while he addressed the chores at hand.

Sitting on the bench outside the shop to enjoy the crisp afternoon air of a cloudy day, Robert studied the sleeve of his father's shirt that would have covered his arm, had he still possessed the missing limb. Becky had sewn the loose sleeve to the side of the shirt, as she had done with all of his shirts. "Father?"

"Yes, lad." Peter sat beside Robert on the bench, aware that *something* was on his son's mind.

"Why did you lose your arm?"

Peter responded with his first thought. "The coal mine is a greedy mistress, my boy. She takes all you have to give her, and even then it is not enough—so she takes your mind and body."

"I don't mean that, Father. I mean, why did God let it happen? Every day when you were in the mine, mother would pray for you to come back safe to her. So why did God let the mine cave in on you?"

Peter paused, realizing his son was asking a much more theological question than he had first thought. Somberly, he responded, "I don't know why God does the things He does, or even why He lets things happen that He could have otherwise prevented. What I *do* know is that He has a plan for us—and to make that plan work, sometimes it *seems* as though He is working against us."

Robert looked at some straw by his feet, contemplating the somewhat confounding words he was hearing, as his father continued. "I tell you, lad, what I believe in my gut." Robert turned to face his father, waiting for the words that would settle his confusion. "Had I not been hurt in the mine, we would never have moved to London. Therefore, I believe something very special is waiting for us here. Maybe not for me, but most certainly for you, Robert. I believe that one day you will do great things, and all of this will make sense. We don't have to understand it. For now, it's enough that we just accept it."

Robert returned his gaze to the straw on the dirt floor, nodding as he pondered his father's explanation. Wishing to continue this private moment he was sharing with his father, he asked a question that had been weighing on his mind, "Father, are we poor?"

Again, Peter hesitated to consider his son's inquisitive mind before responding. "Wealth is measured in love and friendship, not by the weight of a man's coin purse. I have you and you have me. Together, we have your mother and sister. Every day, we meet new people and make new friends. Nay, son, we are not poor. On the contrary, I would say we are the wealthiest family I know."

Robert smiled, closing his eyes to bask in the warmth of the afternoon sun, as it broke through the clouds to bathe his face in light.

Robert was with his father at the blacksmith's shop one chilly Saturday morning in mid-October, when Peter asked him to help steady a mare so he could shoe her. The warmth from the shop furnace that heated steel hot enough to be forged into nails and shoes was a welcome relief to the boy, who had walked to the stable in the quite brisk morning wind. The shop was quiet, as the dawn broke with only the sound of a single hammer striking the red hot shoe bent over an anvil. Robert watched through a window as the blacksmith's son, Aaron, who was a couple of years older than he, walked a gelding from the barn toward a stall on the opposite side of the shop from where his father worked. Steam shot from the horse's nostrils in dual plumes, like two miniature clouds, rhythmically moving with the horse's head, bobbing up and down, as he walked across the well beaten path.

"Bring me the nail puller and nipper, son," Peter instructed. Robert enjoyed helping his father around the shop. He felt particularly useful when Peter would tell the blacksmith, "I'd rather have Robert here than the arm I left at the bottom of the mine."

Robert handed the tools to his father, took hold of the bridle, and began gently stroking the horse's neck. Peter pulled her right hind hoof between his legs, readying the mare for her shoeing. Just as he relaxed his hold on her leg to reach for the nail puller, a loud pop from the furnace spooked her. She pulled her hoof free, shifted her weight to her front legs and kicked with her hind legs.

Robert watched in horror as his father was sent flying into the workbench behind the mare. "Father!" Robert cried, as he dropped the bridle and let the mare retreat to the far side of the stall. Approaching his father, who lay in a contorted position beneath the bench, Robert had little sense as to how he should help.

Peter held his hip and winced in agony. "Robert, go get help," was all he could manage before losing consciousness. While Robert was extremely grateful his father was alive, as the boy ran in tears for the blacksmith, he could not stop wondering, once again, *Why are these horrible things happening to Father?*

When Peter was examined by a local doctor, it was determined the horse's kick had catapulted him so hard into the workbench that his femur had shattered near the hip socket. Without money for medical care or the technology to repair such a major fracture, he was soon confined to a chair at home.

Never again would Peter walk with his son, stand to greet his wife, or hold employment. This fact took a great toll upon Robert's father, but his wife knew the Cratchit family had to keep moving on. Becky worked hard, taking in extra laundry jobs when she could find them. And for a while, that sufficed. Soon, though, sooner than any of them anticipated, there just wasn't enough money to provide for a family of four.

Chapter 4

Quite soon after Peter's accident at the blacksmith's shop, the Cratchit's rent payments became partial payments. What little they had was given to Robert, who would walk the sixteen blocks to the office of Scrooge and Marley to pay what they could.

Entering the office of the landlords was terrifying to young Robert. The dimly lit room was musty and dappled with webs, reminding him of a dungeon. The two men were as dated and unkempt as the tattered book stacks that lined the walls. Both men wore a ponytail which did little to deter from frowns that elongated the wrinkles in their crotchety old faces. A most ominous pair.

The first month, young Robert tried explaining to the landlords that his father was lame and unable to work, but he was simply handed a piece of paper reporting the total of his father's financial debt and told to leave their office. Upon returning home, Robert handed the paper to his father, who just sat and stared glumly at the numbers on the paper.

The following month, Robert did not ask the landlords for special consideration, but half-hoped they might see the need in his face. Once again, however, a report of his father's growing debt was shoved across the desk at him and he was bade to leave. From that point onward, the boy performed his assigned task without expectation or hope.

On one such visit, though, months later, Robert stepped into the office to make a partial rent payment, only to discover the office vacant. "Hello?" Robert called out into the empty office. "Anyone 'ere?" In the silence that followed, he cautiously stepped into the inner office where Scrooge and Marley kept their desks within arm's reach of each other. Neither man was anywhere to be seen.

Looking around their spartan office, with its tall bookshelves and old, worn out furnishings, Robert's attention was captured by a stack of coins on Scrooge's desk. "Hello?" he said in a quieter voice, this time directing his greeting at the coins. Vividly feeling the despair of his family's poverty, Robert cast all thought of consequences to the wind, quickly glanced around the office to confirm no one was around, and lifted the top coin from the stack. Backing away from the desk in an attempt to leave without notice, he froze momentarily, startled by the sound of a heavy metal chain dragging behind a horse-drawn cart down the cobblestone street, just beyond the front of the building.

Realizing he could be caught at any moment, Robert made a stealthy exit, swiftly tiptoeing across the usually creaking wooden floor. In his right hand, he held the rent payment, as yet undelivered. In his left, he held the first coin he would ever call his own. Walking down the street, away from the landlord's office, he dared not glance back, for fear someone would take notice of him—or worse, Scrooge or Marley might see and recognize him, only to remember later that Robert Cratchit had been near the office at the same time a coin went missing.

It was just one coin, Robert consoled himself. *They have so much money! Surely they won't miss just one coin.* Robert tucked the rent money into his right pocket, but clutched his new coin tightly in his left hand. He avoided the main streets, darting through the alleys, until he could mingle with a crowd on the market street. Only then did he stop and open his fist long enough to see what he held in his possession: *a ten shilling coin.*

He had seen ten shillings before. Indeed, in his right pocket, he carried twelve shillings of his father's money for the month's rent.

But never before had he held so much that belonged to *him*. Mesmerized by the significance of his instant wealth, he didn't even see the two boys who suddenly stood on either side of him.

"Blimey, Robert! Where'd you get that?" a rather stout, scruffy boy asked.

Robert took a breath—grateful it was his two friends, William and Thomas—before responding. "I found it. I found it, right 'ere on the street." Robert's lie to William seemed trivial to him, compared to the crime he had just committed.

"Gaw," mumbled William, as he grabbed the coin out of Roberts hand and began to examine it carefully, "Ten shillings!"

Thomas hurried over to Williams side and stared at the treasure. "I can think of a lot of things I could do with it. Yep, put it to some good use, I would."

Put it to some good use? Robert pondered over those words for a brief moment and then retrieved his coin from Williams hand.

"I'll take that back now, if you please!"

"Let's go spend it!" Thomas suggested, hoping to share in Robert's good fortune.

While Robert paused, William jumped in. "Yes, Robert! Let's go 'ave us something sweet to eat! I'm truly starved, I tell you!"

In a flash, Robert realized the safest way to avoid getting caught with money that was not his was indeed to spend it with his friends.

The three boys ran through the crowd to a nearby bakery, where they bought pastries and tarts. Carrying them outside, they sat down on the brick walkway next to the shop and happily devoured every morsel. With the leftover change, Robert and his friends sought out a street vendor who filled a pocket of each boy with a full scoop and a half of roasted chestnuts. After an hour or so of toasting their good fortune to have a friend like Robert, William and Thomas left for home. Robert bid them farewell, saying, "I 'ave to go to old Scrooge and Marley's, now, to pay rent. Later, mates."

Robert walked slowly back toward the landlord's office. His belly was full, but his heart felt disturbed and strangely empty. Nervous thoughts flooded his mind, as he realized how difficult it might be to keep from being found out. *What if Scrooge or Marley are looking around the office for the missing coin? What if they ask me if I was in their office earlier in the day? What if someone saw me leaving and told them?*

The frightened boy began imagining he would be sent to prison, or worse. His poor parents had suffered so much, yet word that their son, 'the thief,' was in prison would certainly devastate them. *Why?* Robert confronted himself. Aloud now, he asked himself, "*Why* did I do it?"

He stopped in his tracks, only to realize he was standing in front of the bottom step leading to the office of Scrooge and Marley. Robert felt shorter than usual, as he gazed up to see the business sign hanging above him. Although he had walked quite slowly, his breathing was rapid, as though he had run the entire way.

Upon entering the office for the second time of the day, Robert cautiously approached the desks of the two men, both of whom were in their seats. "Good afternoon, Mr. Scrooge, Mr. Marley," he said, greeting the men with a nervous voice. Pulling the rent from his right pocket, he laid the coins on Mr. Scrooge's desk.

The stack of coins, from which he stole earlier, was gone. Neither man seemed particularly agitated. Neither man confronted him about their missing ten shilling piece. The only occurrence— or lack thereof—that may have made this visit unusual was that Mr. Marley didn't bother to hand Robert a piece of paper with the tally of his father's debt. He was simply dismissed by Mr. Scrooge with a somber, "Good afternoon, Mr. Cratchit."

Something, most assuredly, was not right, nagged Robert's intuition as he closed the office door behind him.

As he made his way through the crowd down the hectic London streets, his stomach began to ache from the combination of delicacies he had recently enjoyed at the expense of Mr. Scrooge and Mr. Marley. With a pitiful groan, he stopped and leaned back against the sooty bricks of a hardware store. Gently rubbing his belly to sooth the dull pain, Thomas' words rang out like steeple bells. *Put it to good use, I would.*

"What have I done?" Robert whispered under his breath, lowering his eyes in disgrace.

He groaned again as his stomach rumbled under his hand. The guilt, he feared, would haunt him the rest of his life.

Six days later, after six months of growing debt, when the interest on the debt Marley tracked became larger than the monthly rent, a constable came to the Cratchit's home. The tall, uniformed man was polite and respectful to all, as he stepped into their humble flat. Robert watched from across the room, as the constable handed his father a piece of paper. Peter's eyes closed in silent resolve, as he realized his fate. After just a moment of studying it, he handed the paper to Becky, who cupped her hand over her mouth and broke into tears. Robert sat quietly and stared, as his mother kissed his father and told him that somehow, she would "fix it." Lizzy understood better than Robert what was unfolding before their eyes. She stood silently next to her brother, holding his hand, as two men came in their home and lifted Peter, to carry him outside and set him on the flat bed of a wagon.

"Sorry, Mum", whispered the constable, respectfully tipping his hat to Becky and closing the door behind himself. For a moment, she stood there in silent disbelief at what had just happened. Then, she quickly made her way to a chair at the table and wailed, her body shaking in near convulsions. Both children ran crying to their mother's side, mainly because *she* was. "Mother?" Lizzy asked through her own tears.

Becky could not stop sobbing, but managed to compose herself well enough to comfort her children with a hug. "Lizzy, Robert, your father has been arrested, because we haven't enough to pay our rent. The landlord wants his money, so your father must go to prison until the debt is paid."

Robert sat dumbfounded as the situation crept over him. Lizzy replied, "But, if we 'ave no money, how will we get Father back?"

Becky's composure changed, as she breathed deeply and raised herself up, wiping the tears from her cheeks. "Now you listen to me, both of you," she said, lifting the chin of both children, "I will do *whatever* it takes to pay our debt and bring your father home. I promised your father, as I promise each of you. I will work night and day if I have to."

"As will I," Lizzy added.

"As will I," Robert agreed.

A day later, Peter sat (only because he could not stand) before the local magistrate, professed that he was unable to pay his debt to the office of Scrooge and Marley, and was sentenced to debtor's prison until such time that his debt was paid.

Later that same day, Robert went with Becky to plead to their landlord for Peter's release. What they received, instead, was an eviction notice. After stepping out of the office, Robert watched his mother's hand tremble, as she stared at the notice. Her face was ghostly blank, as if for the first time in his memory, he realized she'd been defeated. "Mother, what does it say?"

Becky snapped back to consciousness, ready to resume her role as mother and protector. "It just says we must find a different place to live, Robert. That's it. We will find a new home. We'll be alright, don't you worry."

But *worry* was what he saw in his mother's eyes, despite her brave words and attempted smile. Believing what his father had recently told him, that he was "the man of the family, now," Robert felt he just had to do something more, if he could. Mustering up his courage, he went back into the landlord's office, where he stood before the two men, holding in his anger and speaking as properly and respectfully as he knew how. "Please, your kind sirs. Please, don't kick my mother, my sister, and me to the streets."

"Be gone!" exclaimed Mr. Scrooge, Robert flinching in response. It actually saddened the old miser somewhat that this boy who carried a few shillings to him at the first of every month would not be coming around anymore. He had grown accustomed to the routine, the boy's thin little face, his miserable poverty; but business was business.

Robert stood his ground, as his legs trembled in fear. "Please, your honorable sirs, I can clean, run errands, anything you like, night and day."

"Out with you, before I break this cane across your beggar's back!" yelled Mr. Marley, as he stood and lifted his walking stick above his head.

Still, Robert stood his ground, although he briefly wondered if he was about to become crippled like his father. "I can count!" he desperately replied. "I can count and I can write!"

Marley backed down, returning to his seat silently, slowly. Scrooge looked at his partner, surprised he did not strike the boy with his cane as he had threatened. "What think ye?" Marley inquired of Scrooge, in more of a business tone.

"Think? Think about what?" Scrooge snapped back.

Robert stood by silently, as the two partners carried on with the conversation as though he wasn't present.

"A clerk," replied Marley. "An apprentice clerk."

"I'm not paying this urchin to ruin our business," Scrooge growled, pointing his finger at Robert.

"We don't have to! He works for us and we let his mother stay in the flat." Both men knew they would be hard-pressed to rent the rat-infested sewer hole to anyone else. Both men knew their business was growing beyond their means to track their accounts without working long into the night. Both men knew they were facing a fine opportunity.

"Boy! Fetch your mother and stand before me," Scrooge exclaimed, as he turned his attention back to Robert. "Make haste!"

Robert ran back through the front door of the building to where his mother stood just outside. She had been close enough to hear the men yelling at her son, but unable to follow the conversation.

"Come, Mother, come," Robert urged, as he pulled on Becky's arm. Though she trusted her boy's moral fortitude, her fear of what these men were capable of made it difficult for her to move. Within a matter of moments, though, she was standing next to Robert in front of the twin desks, pulling at the cloth she had been using to wipe her tears.

Together they stood in silence as Scrooge pinned a note, ignoring the mother and son before him. As he finished writing, he shook the remaining ink from his quill into the inkwell before returning it to its holder.

Slowly Scrooge looked up from his work and spoke in a somewhat more subdued voice, as his partner leaned back with a grin to watch the meeting proceed. "I—uh, that is we, my associate and I . . ." Even though Scrooge saw Becky as a class beneath him, he still could not get past his upbringing to talk respectfully to a lady, no matter what her social standing. "That is to say, Mr. Marley and myself have a proposition we wish to discuss." Becky nodded, trying her best to muster a smile for the men who just that very morning had her crippled husband sent to prison for doing nothing worse than being lame and poor.

Scrooge continued with a more formal speech pattern. "The firm of Scrooge and Marley is willing to take on the young lad here," he said, gesturing toward Robert, "as our apprentice. In return for his service, you will be allowed to remain at your current residence." Becky let out a gasp, not realizing she had been holding her breath since she stood before the men. She quickly covered her mouth with her hands, for fear her emotions, too, would escape.

"The lad's service," Scrooge continued, "will cover your rent. In return, he will sign a contract as will you, his parent, Mrs. Cratchit, promising to remain in apprenticeship until his program is complete. Additionally, he will promise two years service for every year of his apprenticeship. In other words, for every year Mr. Marley and I spend our precious time teaching the boy, he will work in our employment unless we dismiss him sooner." He then took on a more ominous tone as he raised his hand to point his finger at Becky and then at Robert. "But mark my words, the both of you. This arrangement in no way forgives your family's indebtedness to this firm."

Both the mother and her child stood before him terrified, as evident from the wide-eyed stare he received in return for his having made his conditions perfectly clear.

Marley leaned forward to clean up the details. "The lad will be here no later than nine o'clock sharp, six days a week, and work until such time that Mr. Scrooge or myself dismisses him at the end of the day."

"Yes, yes, your kind sirs," Becky gratefully replied.

Scrooge turned the contract of apprenticeship, which he was penning, to face the Cratchits. He dipped his quill and handed it to Becky who signed first, followed by Robert's signature under his mother's. After blotting the ink on the contract and returning the quill, he shooed her toward the door with a wave of his hand. "Well, be gone then. The two of you have troubled me enough for one day."

Robert turned back to the two business owners before following his mother through the door, and remembering his manners, said, "Your servant, Mr. Marley."

Marley responded with an automatic, "Your servant."

With that, Robert turned his attention to his other new employer and said in kind, "Your servant, Mr. Scrooge."

Scrooge stopped himself short, contemplating the words of an otherwise polite greeting between two gentlemen. Indeed, the words had more meaning in the case of his new apprentice. Altering his response to lay the tone for Robert's apprenticeship, he muttered, "Yes, yes, you are, and best you don't forget it!"

Marley leaned back in his chair, smiling at his partner, of whom he was proud for stating the obvious, wishing he had been quicker to make the connection himself.

Robert nodded his head in acceptance and turned to join his mother outside. The walk home was filled with his mother's praise for her fine young man of business, who had just saved his family's home. But Robert could only half-listen, as he dwelled on Scrooge's words and his own imagined sense of how different his life was about to become.

Given his fulltime position as an apprentice clerk, Robert was no longer able to attend school. "You know, your apprenticeship is now your school," Becky explained to her young, hardworking son later that night during dinner.

"Yes, Mother, I realized that when we were standing in their office."

"But, this does not mean you stop learning," she continued. "Your entire life will be a learning experience. You and I will continue your studies in the evenings after dinner – agreed?"

"Agreed," Robert replied somewhat solemnly. *I wasn't concerned about the schoolwork*, he thought to himself. *It's my friends, actually, who I'm going to miss.*

He watched as the troubled look on his mother's face softened to a faint smile. Flashing her a toothy grin, he added, "Why, I'll be the best clerk in all of London, I will!"

Laughing, Becky reached across the small table and patted his hand. "Yes, you will, my love. Yes, you will!"

Chapter 5

No matter how early he awoke, it seemed Robert always needed to run to the office to be there on time. Past the man on the corner who begged for bread, past the woman who left her door open to sweep out her shop, turning corner after corner, until the old building came into view, the one with the large hanging sign that could have easily read, 'Scrooge and Marley *and Servant.*'

He copied ledgers and learned to total figures that were given to him in writing and sometimes verbally. Poor penmanship, mistakes, and accidents were often met with a strike from a cane that Scrooge kept propped in a corner near the desk where Robert worked. Sometimes the punishment was a blow to his hand, while others were multiple lashings on his back. Still, Robert worked on, knowing his work kept a roof over his mother and sister, as well as himself.

Early on, he learned the harsh, miserly ways of his employers went far beyond his own treatment or that of his family. In a mid afternoon, not unlike most other afternoons, the door opened and a rather portly old gentleman stepped into the business. He wore an overcoat that may have fit him once, but no longer possessed the capacity to button before him. Robert quickly hopped down from the stool behind his writing desk and approached the potential client as he had been trained. "Good afternoon, sir," he said as he held his hand out to accept the gentleman's top hat and coat.

With a pleasant smile and glimmer in his eyes, the man replied, "My, what a fine gentleman you are." After placing a hand on the young clerk's shoulder, he asked, "May I inquire if Mr. Scrooge might be available?"

Although Scrooge and Marley could easily hear any conversation from their outer office and entryway, neither would acknowledge a visitor until he was properly introduced.

"Yes sir, he is here. Who shall I announce?" Robert asked with a rehearsed response.

Following a jolly laugh, the gentleman replied only, "My fine fellow, believe me, your master knows me fine and well. Just tell him an old friend requests a minute of his time."

Robert nodded, smiling in response to the man's infectious good nature, and preceded the visitor directly into the inner office where he stood before the desks of his employers, "Pardon me Mr. Scrooge, Mr. Marley."

"Yes, what is it?" Scrooge replied in his usual gruff voice, without lifting his eyes from his work.

"A gentleman to see you, Mr. Scrooge. He says he is an old friend and asks for a minute of your time."

"Friend? What friend?" Scrooge replied with a voice that could have just as easily been that of Mr. Marley.

Scrooge was the first to look up, and right away recognized the gentleman who was now standing in the doorway to their office. "Mr. Fezziwig, as I live and breathe!" Scrooge stood and scurried past Robert to shake the hand of his former employer, but Marley kept his position, leaning back in his chair to observe the situation of which he was acutely suspicious.

Although polite to his old friend and mentor, Scrooge presented a cold demeanor to his apprentice clerk when he pushed past Robert and said, "You can go now, boy." The sudden change in personality did little to impress Mr. Fezziwig, and in truth, gave him cause for embarrassment for the young clerk who he had so fondly greeted.

"Please be seated," Scrooge suggested as he returned to his own chair, behind his own desk.

"Yes, what brings you to our office after all these years?" Marley inquired with a hint of mistrust.

"My, the two of you have certainly done well by yourselves," Fezziwig began as he looked around the office. Even though the office was dank and dismal, he could tell by the size of the ledgers on the bookshelf that business had grown steadily through the years.

"Yes... we do our best," Scrooge said as he saw the calculating mind he knew so well perform a quick audit. "But how may we serve you, sir?"

"And what a fine gentleman, your clerk," Fezziwig continued, nodding toward Robert in the outer room who was trying to look busy, but easily overheard every word of the business meeting. "I am certain he will be a great asset to your business one day. You were not much older than he, when I took you under my wing, as it were," Fezziwig said toward Scrooge.

Scrooge and Marley looked at one another, both men recognizing the approaching plea for money from a man who had little to offer in return.

"Quite a turn of events, wouldn't you say," Fezziwig said with a nervous laugh. "One day, you coming to me seeking your own apprenticeship, and now, here I am coming to you much as you did me."

As if it were a coordinated move, Scrooge and Marley simultaneously leaned back in their chairs with their arms crossed before them, waiting for Fezziwig to answer Scrooge's last question.

Fezziwig studied the cold expressionless faces of the two men. There was a time when Ebenezer Scrooge was a jovial spry young lad. Now though, he realized he was not dealing with the young man he once knew, or at least, not as he once knew him. With the smile he always carried, but without the laughter, he asked the question that got to the heart of his visit, "Gentlemen, I've... I've come here this fine day, to invite you to participate in a business venture, for which I endeavor to raise capital and secure the necessary funds to launch operations these coming months."

Scrooge and Marley remained stone-faced.

When Fezziwig realized neither man was going to flinch, he continued, "I... that is, my partners and I seek to raise fourteen thousand pounds, and by investing early, I will be able to assure you a substantial percentage of ownership."

"And, with what resources do you intend to secure such a sizable loan?" Marley asked with a less than enthusiastic response.

"Well, I... I don't have the collateral for the loan, which is why we are offering part-ownership."

"We already own a business," Scrooge said, with a similar monotone response.

"Gentlemen, if I may explain the nature of the business, I'm sure you will be excited to..."

"We are not interested in the nature of your business," Scrooge added coarsely.

"But, Mr. Scrooge," Fezziwig pursued, "I thought for certain, after the years we worked together, you would at least hear me out."

"What we shared in the past, Mr. Fezziwig, was a business arrangement. You paid a day's salary for every day I served you; nothing more... nothing less. In due time, we parted ways; nothing lost... nothing gained. A clean slate, as it were sir. Today you come here with a business proposal that is unfavorable to both me and my partner. Simply put, we reject your offer."

"Mr. Scrooge!" Fezziwig protested. "Surely you learned better lessons than this as my apprentice. You yourself observed one fine day how every man of business who entered our shop was treated with respect and dignity. The more humble the man, the more pleasant his visit. Surely you recall, Mr. Scrooge."

"I recall the hours you wasted with penniless patrons, Mr. Fezziwig."

"Not a moment of time that is devoted to charity is a moment wasted, Mr. Scrooge. Respecting my fellow human beings was the *making* of me," Fezziwig continued.

"The *breaking* of you, you mean," Scrooge countered.

"You fear the world, Mr. Scrooge. Is this what you endeavor to teach your young apprentice?" Fezziwig protested, motioning to Robert in the outer room.

Scrooge leaned forward as he prepared his final assault on his former master. "I *loathe* the world, Mr. Fezziwig. I was ill equipped to compete in business when I left your firm. If I seem hardened to you, it is because I have scrapped and fought for every penny I have, against men who were weaker than me. And yes, I teach my clerk to trust no one. I teach him to pick himself up when he is knocked down and to try harder next time. I teach him all the things I should have learned from you, but didn't!"

"Mr. Scrooge! Why, I never…!" Fezziwig exclaimed, overtaken by a loss of words.

Scrooge held his position, staring at the man he once loved as a father, while Marley leaned forward to retrieve his quill and resume his writing, but not before concluding, "This meeting has come to a close. Good day, Mr. Fezziwig."

Fezziwig looked back and forth between the two men, particularly to Mr. Scrooge who was once like a son to him as well, searching his memory for a thought or idea he could offer to sway the conversation in his favor, but found nothing in their callousness. Slowly he stood, realizing he must take his leave, and that their relationship is not as it once was, and never will be, "Good day, Mr. Scrooge, Mr. Marley. Perhaps one day, we will meet under more favorable circumstances."

Neither Scrooge nor Marley responded. Scrooge watched his former mentor turn to let himself out. As he walked past Robert, who had seen many men before this one, walk out with rejected purpose, he offered his own advice, "Be careful, lad. Evil begets evil."

Chapter 6

Sunday was the only opportunity for the family to visit Peter. Robert looked forward to the visits with cautious apprehension. That is, during the week, he remembered the father who could out-work any man in the mines, a father who was bigger than life. On Sunday, however, he visited a crippled shell of the man who once was. Although this would unnerve Robert somewhat, still, it brought a palpable joy to him just watching his father light up seeing his family in the visitation yard.

After kissing his wife and children, Peter would often just smile quietly, staring at them in deep gratitude for their coming to see him. Peter never asked about the balance of the debt. He knew how much his good wife earned and what the expenses were to provide a meager living for the three of them. Becky paid the court all she could afford, usually a shilling or two per month, trying to pay down Peter's debt. However, both of them knew her efforts had little impact.

He was as proud of Robert for the work he did to keep a roof over the family as the young man was ashamed of working for the men who had his father locked away for his misfortunes. "My, how you grow," Peter said, during one visit soon after Robert had begun his apprenticeship. "Your mother and I could not be prouder of your position in a business firm. You will be quite the man about town one day, I'm sure."

Robert relished his father's attention, yet felt less the man than his father boasted about.

During each successive visit, Robert noticed his father coughing more often and seeming thinner. "I imagine the day will come soon," he said, trying to uplift his father's spirit, "when we can go fishing together again, Father." Hearing his son's words, Peter forced a smile, but could not reply.

Having been told by his mother that residents in a debtor's prison are allowed to receive food and carry tools, Robert pulled out a small knife and laid it on the table in front of him. He then took out two apples from the bag of food Becky brought along. One apple was the perfect shape and color, twice the size of the other one, which was small and knotty with brown spots.

"Which should we eat, Robert?" Peter asked, after examining the fruit.

"Let's eat the big juicy one, Father," Robert replied, looking forward to sharing a treat.

Peter cut a slice from the big apple and handed it to Robert, who ate it without hesitation. He then cut an equal size piece from the small, knotty apple and handed it to him, as well. Robert ate the slice and stopped, as his eyes grew wider, "Father, this apple is so much sweeter than the first."

"Good lad!" Peter then held both apples up in his hand for Robert to see. "Remember, son, do not judge a man by the way he looks or the tree from which he came. It's what is *inside* a man that matters most." As usual, Robert listened with rapt attention to his father's utterances, knowing deep in his heart the profound truth of what he was hearing.

Becky and Lizzy, too, appreciated listening to the father-and-son shared dialogue, regardless of their lack of direct involvement. It was gratifying for both to simply be around Peter, who obviously enjoyed the opportunity to share something of the 'usual routine' with his family. Indeed, with the parting kiss at the end of each two-hour visitation, Becky wondered, week after week, if she would even see her husband alive on the next.

Besides being permanently maimed and crippled, Peter's constant cough revealed the all too familiar signs of 'black lung,' the disease so common among coal miners who had spent the better part of their lives inhaling coal dust. Given the amount of time Peter had been a miner, Becky was not surprised that his shortness of breath increased, as well as the severity of his hacking cough. His continually declining lack of energy, too, troubled her deeply. Still, she continued putting on her best face with each visitation, praying always for a turnaround in her husband's health.

Four Sundays later, Becky stood in the prison yard with her children and a cloth-wrapped bundle containing her homemade rolls. "Looking for Peter Cratchit, are ye'?" came the voice of a man approaching her from behind.

Becky turned to greet the man. "Yes, sir, do you know where he is?"

Directing her with a shift of his eyes and nod of his head to the small building across the yard, opposite the housing unit, he replied, "He's in the sick house. You can go ask for 'im, if you want, but you wouldn't catch me going in there."

The trio walked directly over to the 'sick house,' and, curious to Becky, no one stopped them, as they entered the building. When they stepped into the main hall, they immediately began searching for Peter, wondering which bed he occupied. Becky wasn't certain, but when a man in the third bed down from them coughed, she finally recognized the frail man as her husband. "We're here, my love." she whispered, bending down to kiss Peter's sweaty forehead.

Feebly, he half-opened his sunken eyes and stared blankly at his wife. Robert and Lizzy moved closer to the bed and looked on with shock at the alarming condition of their father. Peter was now a skeleton of a man. His ribs showed through his skin, as his chest slowly raised and lowered with each labored breath.

Seeing Robert standing at the foot of his bed, Peter motioned for him to come closer. Leaning in toward his father, the boy listened attentively, as Peter spoke softly into his son's ear.

Robert responded with a somewhat perplexed look on his face, but said, "Thank you, Father. I'll remember."

When Becky noticed Peter mouthing some words, she bent down, bringing her ear next to his dry, cracked mouth. "What is it, my dear?" she whispered.

After some labored words to his wife, he closed his eyes and fell into a deep sleep. When they walked out, Lizzy put her arm around her mother's waist. "What did Father say?"

Becky stopped and turned to face her two children, with tears beginning to pool in her eyes, "He said he will love us always."

Then Becky asked the same of her son. "What was it your father told you, Robert?"

Robert thought for a moment, wanting to make sure he repeated his father's words verbatim. "He said, 'Butterflies are caterpillars that have been set free.' I dare say I cannot imagine what he was trying to tell me."

Robert and Lizzy then began to cry, and their mother pulled them into her arms. The three huddled there together for a few moments, hugging each other tightly, as a cold drizzle began to fall.

Later that very week, less than a year into his imprisonment, Becky received word that Peter had died from pneumonia—his frail condition and charred lungs had left him powerless to fight the infection.

The message informed the Cratchit family that the remains of Peter Cratchit were properly buried in the prison graveyard, marked only with the number 6970. There was never an option for the family to claim or view the body. No opportunity for a religious burial. The prison graveyard, by order of the local magistrate, was off limits to the public.

Faithful husband, father, and servant, Peter Cratchit existed no more. The population had decreased by one.

Alone in the basement flat, Becky took Peter's coat from the hook near the front door and held it tightly, as she curled up in bed to begin a lengthy cry. The coat still smelled of horses and sweat from his days at the blacksmith's. She could smell in the sweat on the coat the scent of the man she loved, and now had lost.

When Lizzy and Robert came home, they found their mother in her bed, still clinging to Peter's coat. Lizzy asked the question, even though both children already knew the answer, "Mother? Is it Father?"

Becky nodded her head, unable to speak the words, for fear that hearing them spoken, even by her, would make the situation more real. Lizzy crawled into bed next to her mother and began stroking her mother's hair, adding her tears to a blanket that was already soaked with her mother's.

Robert turned his back on his mother and sister, and ran from the bedroom to his bed roll in the corner of the main room. Though he needed his mother's touch and comfort more now than ever before, Robert chose to be alone. His tears fell, as he remembered the kindness and wisdom of his father. Over and over, he heard the last words his father spoke to him; *Butterflies are caterpillars that have been set free.*

Fear interrupted his grief, when he realized he had never known a moment of life without his father. *What's life going to be like without Father around?* he wondered anxiously. *For me—and for all of us?* Reaching into his pocket, he pulled out his only possession that had once been his father's: a small wood-handled knife his father had given him one day while helping him at the blacksmith shop. Over and over, Robert stuck the knife into the wood floor, released it to stand alone, and then pulled it out to do it again.

The strain on the small family of three was tremendous. Charity was scarce in such hard times, yet Becky never missed an opportunity to buy slightly spoiled food at highly reduced prices, whenever she could find it. Occasionally, too, a fellow worker at the laundry would offer up some hand-me-down garment her own child had outgrown, for which Becky would be deeply grateful to receive.

At the beginning of one now typically quiet meal, during which the three Cratchits dared not speak of Peter's passing, Robert stared at the all-too-familiar bowl of cabbage and potatoes set in front of him. With a brief grimace, he conveyed his dissatisfaction with the tiresome stew. Fortunately, Becky's homemade rolls presented at least one appetizing morsel on the table. With one quick grab, he reached over and took the roll sitting next to Lizzy's bowl to add to his own. Lizzy lashed back, "Robert!" snatching her roll back from his greedy hands, followed by a shove on his shoulder.

Robert responded as if by reflex and struck her jaw hard with the back of his left hand. Before Lizzy could even gasp, Becky slammed her wooden spoon on the table, stood up, and yelled, "Robert! Have you lost your mind? How dare you strike your sister! You apologize this instant, young man!"

Though knowing he was on the wrong side of this argument, Robert lashed back without a moment of self-control. "I want more damn bread!" he insisted, with a childish tone that surprised even himself.

"You want more bread, you ask!" Becky responded.

"I am the reason you two have a home!" Robert hollered, knowing he was digging a hole too deep.

"And I am the reason you have a life!" Becky fired back. In an instant, she leaned forward and roughly grabbed her son's arm, pulling him away from the small wooden table and forced him backwards into the corner of the room. "You stand right here, young fellow, until you are ready to talk and behave like a gentleman."

Rubbing the tender spot on his arm left by his mother's grasp, Robert did as he was told, but glared into her eyes with deep disdain. Becky turned away from him with a frustrated grunt and returned to her chair at the table across from Lizzy, who was still massaging the soreness from her cheek. Furrowing his brow, Robert watched his sister. "I didn't strike her that hard," he muttered, lowering his gaze to the floor and kicking at a loose board in the floor.

"Eat up, Liz," Becky said in a voice that strained to impress some semblance of mothering affection, hiding her disappointment in Robert. The rest of the meal was silent, as Robert stood in place watching the two women eat.

Becky cleared the table, leaving Robert's bowl next to a single piece of bread and his cup of water. Robert continued stewing in his puddle of half-spent anger, as Lizzy moved her chair by the window where she could stitch some holes in a basket of clothing, while Becky filled a wash basin to clean the dinner dishes.

A steady rain began falling on the old city. The damp, gray evening matched Robert's cranky, sullen mood. As he stood by the small window, he watched the rain hit the puddles in the ruts of the cobblestone street. Eventually, the scene before him carried Robert out of the pit in which he felt mired, and his mind drifted back to a happier time, a time when his father was alive and he could just be the child. Such was a time, he recalled, when nothing was demanded from him, when he could run barefoot and carefree in the tall grass near his home in Bristol.

As Robert was remembering the happier times of the fishing trips and long talks with his father, a wagon rolled by, dragging a heavy chain, and hit a deep puddle. The clanking of the chain startled Robert, as it seemed to him the same sound he heard after he stole the money from Scrooge. He watched the water in the puddle slosh from the impact, before it once again became a smooth surface, broken only by the steady pounding of the rain.

The countless raindrops made ripple after ripple in the puddle. And then it all came together in a flash. Robert remembered his father's lesson, and his young mind began to understand how his actions had changed his world:

I stole from Scrooge, and then Scrooge had my father arrested. And now this--Father is dead, yet he was also Mother's husband and Lizzy's father, as well. So many people hurting because of the ripple I caused when I stole the money. And for what? Just a few tasty treats to share with my friends!

Robert looked at his sister and his mother. Just an hour earlier, all three were happy and talking. Sure, their life had been hard. But Robert now saw how his anger and temper had changed the room. Neither his mother nor his sister was happy. His actions had *rippled* out and hurt them once again. And just like the walls of the water pail, their pain bounced back to him.

"Mother?" Robert calmly asked, ready to beg her forgiveness.

Becky froze for a moment, and then wiped her hands dry on her apron. Turning to face him, he could see the tears running down her cheeks. She walked over to her seat at the table. After sitting for a moment, and taking a deep breath, she beckoned Robert to her side. He ran to her, throwing his arms around her neck and weeping uncontrollably. Becky realized, as she held her young man in her arms, the burden he labored under at his apprenticeship, compounded with the loss of his father, was more than a thirteen-year-old boy could bear.

Drying his face with her apron, she listened attentively, as Robert's apology came spilling out. "Mother, I'm sorry! I'm sorry for acting like a hooligan! I'm sorry for swearing! I'm sorry for yelling at you! I'm sorry for hitting Lizzy!" Just then, he turned to his sister, realizing she deserved his apology, as well. Running to Lizzy, he hugged her and she generously returned the gesture. "Oh, Lizzy, I'm so sorry I hurt you! As God is my witness, I will never hurt you again! Please forgive me!"

Returning to his mother's side, he continued with his apology. "I don't know what came over me. I certainly don't mean the things I said. I just can't imagine what Father would do to me right now if he knew I hit Lizzy, or yelled at you, Mother." Looking up through the ceiling toward the heavens, he begged another pardon. "Please forgive me, Father."

"Robert," Becky said in a soothing voice, "I forgive you, as does your father. I have just never seen you act that way before."

Reflecting a moment further, Robert replied, "I think I may have just been mimicking Mr. Scrooge and Mr. Marley, Mother. They yell at me every day and, please forgive me, I just did the same to you." He stopped short of telling her they also regularly whipped him with sticks. He knew she would live on the street before she would ever let them touch him again.

"Robert, we survive only by the grace of God, not by our own fortunes or misfortunes. Scrooge and Marley may be your masters, but please remember I am your mother, and I cannot, and *will* not, tolerate their sort of behavior in this family. We love and respect each other, as well as our friends and neighbors. You know as well as I do, young fellow, your father would never allow us a cross word between ourselves."

"I know for certain, Mother. Please forgive me. I will never raise my voice to you, or to any woman, for that matter, as long as I live. If I were to remember just one thing Father taught me, it would be that we must be happy with what we have, never allowing ourselves to believe we deserve more." Robert turned his attention back to Lizzy, "I'm sorry I took your bread. I truly can't imagine what would possess me to do such a thing."

Lizzy smiled at him, knowing she was in for several good days, or maybe even weeks, of Robert being extra loving and attentive.

Turning back to his mother, Robert realized that very moment he must unburden his soul before the darkness overtook him. "Mother, there's more."

"What is it, my dear?"

"It's my fault! It's all my fault!" Robert buried his face in his mother's shoulder, as tears soaked her sleeve.

"What is Robert? What's wrong?"

"It's my fault Father got arrested! It's my fault he died! It's all my fault!"

"Oh dear, dear! What on *earth* would make you feel you caused this?"

"Mother, I stole some money from Mr. Scrooge. I knew it was wrong when I did it, but I did it anyway. Then, a few days later, Scrooge had Father arrested. Don't you see? It's all my fault!"

Becky pulled Robert's face up with both hands, to make sure she had his attention, "Now, see here, Robert Cratchit! If you stole money from Mr. Scrooge, then you did a very bad thing—but that act, in no way, caused your father's fate. We can blame the coal mine that fell on him, or that old mare for kicking him, but we will never blame ourselves. Do you hear me?"

Robert closed his eyes, ashamed that his mother now knew he was a thief. He nodded in acceptance of her explanation, but the burning guilt in his heart persisted all the same.

"Now, Robert, if you stole from Mr. Scrooge, you must make it right. Do what you must to right the wrong."

"I will, Mother. I promise, I will." Suddenly Robert realized the salvation in forgiveness. If his mother could forgive him, maybe someday he would be able to forgive himself.

"Please, eat your dinner now," she said, motioning to him to return to his chair and eat. "Let's put this day behind us." And with that, Robert re-took his place at the table. Cabbage, potato soup, and a single piece of bread never tasted as good to Robert as they did this night.

Chapter 7

Robert struggled to see through the dark, dusty, dirty air. Ahead of him and beside him, he could barely make out the faint flicker of light from lanterns. Straining to fill his lungs with air, each painful breath ended with a hacking cough. Suddenly, the whole darkened world around him shook with a thunderous rumble, and the roof collapsed, boulders and beams caving in on top of him. The massive weight of the rubble compressed his chest to the point he couldn't breathe. With one last gasp, he reached his free arm past his head. Without warning, two hands grasped his arm and pulled.

Coughing and gasping, he found himself alone in the meadow where he'd often walked home with his father from the mines. In an instant, Robert realized the hands that freed him were those of his father, who now stood next to him. "Father?" Robert inquired, confused by his presence.

"Lad, remember the ripples." With that, Robert sprang straight up in bed, looking from side to side, searching for his father, breathing hard, still feeling the pain in his chest from straining to breathe in the mine. It took him several minutes to lie back down, and even longer to close his eyes.

Robert detested his job most when he was sent out to serve foreclosure notices, and *especially* when he was sent with the paperwork to the magistrate's office to sue a tenant, which generally led to debtor's prison. It made him feel as though he was complicit in his own father's incarceration.

One day while serving a notice of eviction, Robert walked with a heavy heart slowly down the market street, passing the vendors with their food stands and other merchandise for sale or trade. *One could buy just about anything here*, he dreamily thought, *if the funds were in hand.* The multitudes of sounds in the marketplace were abruptly overcome by the whinny of a horse nearly a block away. Robert turned, as did the market patrons, to see a horse—still attached to a nearly empty cart—rearing on his hind legs while kicking with his front. The fear in his eyes, as his ears lay back, gave notice to those close enough to see, the horse was spooked, though it was not obvious what had startled him.

The wheel lock snapped off the cart, as the horse charged down the street in Robert's direction. People hustled out of the center of the road, making a clear path for the runaway horse, save one terrified obstacle. Alone in the street center, a boy half Robert's age stood petrified, as he watched the horse run at full gait in his direction. The cart bounced from one wheel to the other, while pieces broke away, one splintered plank at a time. Only Robert ran against the tide of people, directly into the path of this galloping beast.

Arriving at where the boy stood, Robert grabbed his arm with only an instant to decide whether to continue across the street with the boy in his arms, or to pull him back from whence he came. From the corner of his eye, Robert saw the horse-drawn cart take a leap toward his side of the street, so instinct followed that the next bounce would be away. His good sense took charge, as he pulled the boy toward him and backed up two steps, before forcing the child beneath himself, landing his body on the terrified child.

The horse diverted slightly to miss the children, while the airborne wheel passed directly over their bodies. The young boy's father witnessed the scene unfold from the chemist's shop, where he'd just been a patron. He reached the pair in the street just as

Robert stood the child up to make sure he was unhurt. The man dropped to his knees next to his son to hold the child, who surely would be dead, but for the courageous act of the young lad before him.

Robert started to wander away, pleased that the young boy was safe. "Boy!" the still terrified father called out in Robert's direction. "You, my fine fellow, come back, please!" The crowd around the three dispersed, as each person recanted their version of the scene, sure to be the choice topic of discussion around many a dinner table.

The man took his son into his arms, as he led Robert to a nearby bench. "What is your name, my young hero?" the man asked Robert, beckoning him to sit beside him on a bench.

"Robert Cratchit, sir."

"Well, Mr. Cratchit, I don't know if you realize this or not, but you just quite literally saved the life of my son."

"Oh, no, sir, I just pushed him out of the way. I didn't hurt him, did I?"

The man chuckled. "Not only a hero, but a modest hero, at that! I dare say you are quite the young gentleman. Who are your parents, my fine fellow?"

"Peter and Becky Cratchit of Camden Town," Robert responded, still politely speaking only when spoken to.

"Well, I would like to meet the parents of London's finest citizen and reward them for your bravery. I dare say they would never believe the story coming from you, if you even told it at all."

"No, sir! I mean, thank you, sir, but you see, my father is…" Robert stopped short of telling the truth of his family's situation. "Truly sir, I do not need a reward, more than knowing your son is well."

"Come now, my fine fellow, there must be some way I can offer my gratitude for your heroics."

"For me? Thank you kindly, sir, but no. If, though, you could see your way to help this family, it would relieve me from the burden of committing a terrible deed." Robert looked up directly into the man's eyes, as he pulled the eviction notice from inside his shirt pocket and handed it to him.

"And what burden could such a young gentleman carry?" the man asked, taking the folded piece of paper and opening it.

From the office of Scrooge and Marley

The tenants residing at 115-A Reading Street are hereby evicted from the premises for failure to fulfill the contract of agreement, and are liable for the delinquency of payment for said property to the sum of 18 Shillings and 7 Pence. Failure to pay full restitution will result in civil action.

"Oh, dear," the man said. Looking up from the paper, he asked Robert, "Is this your family?"

"No sir, not mine. I work for Scrooge and Marley as their clerk, and part of my job is to run their errands."

"I see, and you are telling me you would feel rewarded in kind if I help this family instead of your own?"

"I would indeed, sir. It breaks my heart when I have to deliver evictions."

In awe of the young man sitting beside him, the man sat his son down on the bench at his other side and pulled a change purse from his vest pocket. From the purse, he retrieved three coins and placed them in Robert's hands. "Here are thirty shillings. Take these coins to your employer and tell him the back rent is hereby paid, along with the month that follows, and hand him back the notice of eviction, as well. Then, go to the tenants and inform them their rent is paid in full by an anonymous benefactor. Tell them no more than that about me or where you got the resources, agreed?"

"Oh, yes, indeed, sir, I shall!"

"And Mr. Cratchit, my name is Charles McFadden—and this," he said, gesturing to the child beside him, "is my son, Avery. If ever I can be of service to you, you have only to come to the McFadden Mercantile Corporation on the next street, and ask for me. I am now, and forever, your servant, sir—forever with a debt of gratitude for you and the fine family who raised you."

"Thank you, sir, indeed, thank you." With a brief moment's pause and a smile at the little boy snuggled against his father's arm, Robert added, "Pleased to meet you, Master Avery."

Robert turned and began running back down the street to work his way through the alleys, before reaching the office of his employer. As he stepped through the doorway, he recognized this was the first time he had ever felt excited and actually happy to enter the office of Scrooge and Marley.

Standing before the desk of Mr. Scrooge, Robert waited until his master spoke. "Well?" came the all familiar gruff voice, the old man never looking up from the ledger in which he was writing. "Did you deliver the notice?"

"No, sir," Robert replied. Whether it was dangerous or not, he secretly wanted to tease Scrooge into a fit, or at least to watch the veins swell up on his high forehead.

"No? What do you mean 'No'?!"

Robert noticed Mr. Marley had stopped his paperwork alongside of Scrooge, and eagerness in his eyes had emerged. Calmly placing the three silver coins he'd been given on Scrooge's desk, Robert laid the eviction notice down and began recounting his now made-up story he had practiced while running to the office. "They asked me to give you this along with their apology. You see, the master of the house was called out of town for work and only now returned with the rent. They hope you will accept their apology, along with the next month's rent in advance." This may have been a lie, but at the same time, it was a kept promise, according to Robert's way of thinking, and thus deemed necessary.

Scrooge's boney fingers slowly uncurled from the fist he was forming, and he raked in the coins that had been placed on his desk. "Humph, so be it! Get the ledger and mark it paid. Move on then, sir!"

With that, Robert grabbed the ledger and, with a smile that would not leave his face for an hour, marked the ledger *Paid In Full* next to 115-A Reading Street. Following that, he made the same entry for the next month.

At the close of business, Robert made his way to 115-A Reading Street to tell the woman of the household the story, as instructed. He told her he was delivering an eviction notice to her and was stopped by an anonymous benefactor who paid their debt, and another month's rent. The woman broke into tears as she hugged Robert, explaining that her husband was a little behind on his work, but with this generous gift, she was sure they would be able to meet the rent going forward.

Robert's smile returned and lasted on his face long past the time he walked in through the door of his home and greeted his mother and sister.

Chapter 8

Robert had no formal education, but largely due to his mother's teachings, he was more schooled than most boys his age. Working so closely to Scrooge and Marley, he, as well, learned to become quite proficient at maintaining a proper ledger and documenting business transactions. Yet, over the past three years of his apprenticeship with these two, he had also become quite streetwise, as he had learned to solicit help for the less fortunate before himself. Those in need often sought his help, while those with plenty responded to his charm and good heart. Scrooge and Marley knew only that their clerk had an uncanny ability to return with rent and mortgage money, whenever he was dispatched to serve evictions. Since money was always preferable to vacant housing, they never questioned the young clerk's talent.

Robert never sought or accepted a penny for himself or his family from the kind souls who generously donated to the worthy cause of helping the poor and hungry. He knew he had a home and a good family, yet every day he watched as other families were broken apart and forced to sleep in the back alleys, like discarded pets. This seemingly endless scenario inspired him to continue doing what he could to reach out to those with means to help those in need.

Sometimes, though, there was no money available to pay the debts. Still, more often than not, Robert managed to find a way. When two families struggled, he would evict one, under the agreement they would move into the home of another and share expenses. When the choice a family faced was between food and rent, he would bring them meat and potatoes donated by a sympathetic tavern owner or merchant.

Robert continued to work for Scrooge and Marley, as he grew and matured into a young man. For quite some time, the only money the family had was that which Becky and Lizzy brought home from Becky's work as a laundress and Lizzy's ever improving skill as a seamstress. However, soon after her eighteenth birthday, Lizzy married Aaron Madison, the son of the blacksmith for whom her father had previously worked. She moved in with the family of her new husband, as he honed his skills as an apprentice blacksmith. Becky and Robert remained in the flat owned by Scrooge and Marley, living now solely on Becky's income.

Sunday was Robert's day to be with his family. He proudly dressed in his only formal attire, which his mother had rescued and mended from discarded garments that were never claimed from the scrub-house where she worked. Once she was also dressed in her finest and best, Becky and Robert would go to church for morning services. She would hold Robert's arm, as he escorted her, front and center, to the pew where they sat with Lizzy and her husband.

Within the church, Robert's talents for helping the poor and destitute were well-known. Few knew him as an apprentice of Scrooge and Marley; but most knew him as a gentle, honest boy who was quickly becoming a true gentleman in every sense of the word. Becky enjoyed the church socials, but it was her son who impressed the church members the most.

Even as a sixteen-year-old, Robert organized charitable events to aid families in the area who were in most need of support. During one such event, while sorting donated clothing, Robert's eyes met those of a fifteen-year-old girl who was doing the same. Standing next to his mother, he handed her a single shoe. Becky looked at the shoe, and then to Robert, noticing he wasn't paying a bit of attention to what he was sorting.

"Robert, why don't you go introduce yourself?" After a moment of silence, Becky tried again. "Robert?"

"Yes!"

Becky bit her lower lip to try to keep her son from seeing her laugh at his shyness. Again she asked, "Why don't you go introduce yourself?"

Knowing he had failed miserably at hiding his interest in the girl on the other side of the table, who was also standing near her mother, but paying him no never mind, he blushed and sought his mother's approval. "Should I?" He then answered his own question in concert with her nod, "Yes, yes, I should."

With the politeness and formality of a young yet humble aristocrat, Robert approached the young girl's mother with hat in hand, addressing her as though the object of his attention did not exist. "Pardon me, madam, my name is Robert Cratchit. I wonder if I might be introduced to your lovely daughter?"

"Well, aren't you quite the young gentleman? I know a thing or two about the young man named Robert Cratchit. People talk, you know." Then, as if acting out in a play, the woman curtseyed Robert and formally introduced her daughter. "Mr. Robert Cratchit, it is my pleasure to introduce you to my daughter, Emily Watkins."

Poor Emily was completely embarrassed by her mother's grand gesture, but she was quietly thrilled that Robert Cratchit had expressed an interest in meeting her. Robert turned toward Emily and reached his hand for hers. "Miss Watkins, it is a pleasure to meet you."

"Likewise, Mr. Cratchit," she replied, as her hand met his in a delicate handshake.

Becky and Mrs. Watkins peered across the table, nodding at each other in satisfied approval. Neither Robert nor Emily would ever know that this chance meeting was arranged days earlier by two resourceful mothers.

After a year of Sunday courtship, with his mother's steadfast support and approval, Robert approached Emily's mother once again, with hat in hand. Because Emily's father had long passed, and her brother was three years younger, decorum dictated that Mrs. Watkins was the person to whom he should convey his request for Emily's hand in marriage. Again, though, the gesture was merely a formality, as Becky and Mrs. Watkins knew this moment was coming, even before Robert.

As required of an English gentleman, after acquiring the approval of Emily's mother, Robert then, on bended knee, asked the same of Emily herself. To his great delight, she joyfully responded, "Yes!"

Soon after proposing to Emily, Robert mustered the courage to address his employers. "Pardon me, Mr. Scrooge, Mr. Marley, sirs." Standing before their desks, he waited as both men made a long to-do of shaking the ink from their quills and propping them in their holders. Each, as well, took a deep, annoyed breath, before looking up to see their apprentice standing before them in his typical nervous fashion. "I plan to wed—and I was wondering if my apprenticeship might be coming to an end soon, such that there might possibly be a position available for me in your business."

Marley leaned back in his chair to contemplate Robert's request, but Scrooge leaned forward, prepared to address the request with full vigor. "You ungrateful beggar!" shouted Scrooge, his rapid breathing foreshadowing a barrage of insults. "After your shiftless father tried to rob us blind, we took you off the streets, gave your family a home—for *free* I might add—taught you the skills of bookkeeping, and now you have the audacity to stand here and demand that we should pay you?! Remove yourself from this business, sir! I can no longer tolerate the sight of you!" Scrooge promptly shifted position in his chair to turn away from Robert, emphasizing his disgust for the young apprentice.

Robert returned to the outer office to sit behind his writing desk, wondering if he had not only lost the opportunity to marry his beloved Emily, but also lost the home he shared with his mother.

Once again, though, Marley took the high road. He knew Robert Cratchit had brought skills to their company that went beyond bookkeeping. He also realized that he and Scrooge would need to hire two, possibly three men to replace their talented apprentice. Scrooge knew this, as well, but could not tolerate the idea he did not have the upper hand in any business deal, especially when dealing with someone he considered so far beneath himself. Leaning over toward Scrooge, Marley put a hand on his partner's shoulder, as both men looked at the floor, their heads nearly touching.

After a few moments of whispered conversation during which neither man looked at the other, Marley closed their brief "meeting" by drawing in a deep breath and exhaling slowly. He then beckoned Robert to appear before them. "Mr. Cratchit?"

Robert rapidly completed the four steps to place himself once again in front of Mr. Marley's desk, dreading what might come from the conversation. "Yes, sir?" The strength in his voice lied for his vigorously pounding heart, which had swiftly migrated south toward his stomach.

"Mr. Cratchit," Marley began in a business-like voice. "After careful deliberation, my partner and I have decided to offer you a position in our firm at the rate of fifteen shillings a week."

Suddenly Robert's vision of darkness turned to dawn. Elated, he glanced momentarily toward Scrooge, who he could see was sulking and looking only at the paper on his desk.

Marley continued, "In addition, you may continue living at your current residence free of charge, for as long as you are employed with us. Does this sound agreeable to you, sir?"

"Oh yes, yes, indeed! That is most generous of you. Thank you, Mr. Marley. Thank you, Mr. Scrooge."

Marley acknowledged the agreement with a nod. Scrooge remained motionless. "Right, back to work then," Marley stated, bringing a close to the discussion.

Robert clasped both hands, as he turned to resume his duties at his desk. In the distance, he could hear cathedral bells. Smiling quietly to himself, he realized that soon, those bells would ring to announce the wedding of Robert and Emily Cratchit.

At the end of his first week of employment, Scrooge reluctantly handed Robert a ten shilling coin, followed by a five shilling coin. "Lock the door, sir," was Scrooge's only comment, as he left the office for the day.

"Thank you, sir. Thank you very much, indeed," Robert replied, as he studied the first coins he had ever earned.

The next day, after Sunday's church services, Robert walked Emily to a park before escorting her home. "Em', I have some wonderful news," he began, just as they sat down on a low stone bench along the overgrown garden path.

Emily took his hand, "What is it, Robert? Tell me! Don't make me wait!" Though she was smiling, she anticipated otherwise frightful news, since she had not yet gained the ability to read her fiancé's more subtle expressions.

"I am fully employed now, my love! Scrooge and Marley have hired me and I am now earning fifteen shillings a week!" His excitement could not contain his pride.

"Oh, Robert! That *is* wonderful news, indeed! I am so proud of you!" Emily looked both ways down the path, confirmed they were alone, and then kissed him squarely on the lips.

To make sure she comprehended the situation, Robert added, "This means we can marry as soon as you wish, my love."

"Our marriage, our lives together, will be blessed with our love, our faith, and our trust for one another," Emily responded, as though she had rehearsed this speech her whole life. "We begin our lives together with a clean slate. We must be completely open with one another, Robert, before we start this journey. So, I must ask you, my dear, is there anything about your past that gives you shame?"

Robert sat back on the bench, still holding Emily's hand, but stared at a caterpillar on the leaf of a flower on the far side of the path. He reflected on her question earnestly, as he searched his past for any suppressed memories that may have been hiding in dark corners.

After a few moments, he turned to look into the waiting eyes of the love of his life, "Soon after my father died, and I had already entered into the apprenticeship with Scrooge and Marley, I caused an argument with Lizzy and got so mad that I hit her."

With a mothering voice, Emily asked, "And have you made amends with Lizzy? Have you asked for her forgiveness and forgiven yourself, as well?"

"Oh my, yes, most definitely! My mother witnessed the entire episode. I apologized to the both of them, begged their forgiveness and swore I would never hit a woman again, for the rest of my life." Then, he realized Emily might rightfully be wondering if her safety might be at risk sometime in the future. Robert tried to reassure her. "I mean what I said, Miss Watkins. You must believe me. I will never again hit a woman, for as long as I live."

Emily smiled at his honest candor, and realized how difficult it must have been for Robert to bare his soul like this. "I believe you, Mr. Cratchit, and I forgive you, as well. What other indiscretions weigh on you?"

After another pause, Robert looked directly into his beloved's eyes and confessed, "Just before Scrooge and Marley sent my father to debtor's prison, I stole a ten shilling coin from Scrooge's desk, when he wasn't looking. I knew it was wrong then, just as I do now, but the temptation was just too great."

"And for this, Robert, have you made amends with Mr. Scrooge?"

"I told my mother what I had done, and she told me I must make it right. But I have not spoken of it since."

Holding his left hand even tighter, the very hand he'd used to steal the coin, Emily implored, "But you must, my love. You must confess to Mr. Scrooge and return to him that which you took."

"Oh, please don't ask me to do that, Emily. Surely you must know he will not take kindly to me, if he learns of this. I would certainly lose my situation and my home. I would lose everything." Turning even more solemn, he whispered, "Surely, I would lose you."

"Oh Robert, you will never lose me. I am yours until the end of time. But we cannot begin our lives together with any unrepentant sins from your past, *or* mine. Your mother is right, my love. You must make it right. You must!"

After a restless night, Robert began his second week of employment, knowing that it may be his last. Soon after Scrooge and Marley took their seats, Robert once again found himself standing before them, terrified about the consequences of his confession. "Pardon me, Mr. Scrooge, Mr. Marley, may I have a moment of your time?"

"What now?" snapped Scrooge. "You want even more of our hard earned money?"

Robert approached Scrooge's desk and set before him the two coins from his previous week's pay. Scrooge and Marley both looked at the coins, and then at Robert, waiting for an explanation of his action. He took a deep breath and began, "When I was a young lad, before I was even your apprentice, I would bring you the rent from my father. I am here to confess that on one such occasion, I was in your office alone and took a ten shilling piece from your desk, Mr. Scrooge. I wish now to pay you the money I took, with interest, and to beg your pardon and forgiveness."

Silence fell over the office, as the two business partners stared at the young man before them, whose head was bowed in shame. After a few moments, which seemed much longer to Robert, Scrooge pulled a piece of paper from his desk drawer and began writing.

Marley, on the other hand, stood with his cane and walked slowly in front of Robert, keeping his eyes on the young man as he circled behind him. Robert could hear the cane whistle through the air at high speed, before it struck the back of his knees, instantly buckling them, dropping him to the ground. Young Cratchit still was upright, but now he stood on both knees.

"I defended you, but you are nothing more than a common thief!" Marley scolded. The second strike from his cane was across his back, bruising both shoulder blades. "I told my partner you were a good and loyal servant! I convinced him to hire you!" Marley continued with his tirade.

Scrooge interrupted his partner by addressing Robert firmly and directly. "Step this way, Mr. Cratchit," as he summoned him to approach his desk. Scrooge rotated the paper on which he was writing for Robert to see. "You have before you a written confession of your crime."

Robert read the short note as written:

I, Robert Cratchit, do woefully and sorrowfully confess to the crime of stealing ten shillings from the business of Scrooge and Marley.

Scrooge continued, "If you wish to keep your position here, Mr. Cratchit, you will sign this confession. If not, then I will go immediately to the authorities and have you arrested, tried, and convicted. As well, I will immediately evict your family from the home you now occupy. Do you understand, sir?"

Robert nodded, as he leaned forward to accept the quill Scrooge had offered him. With a sullen look, he signed his name below the note. Scrooge continued, as Marley returned to his desk. "And Mr. Cratchit, if you ever cross us again, if you ever leave or lose your position in this firm, I will have no other option than to hand this note to the authorities and seek restitution, have I made myself clear, Mr. Cratchit?" Scrooge stood to lean over the young man, lifted his fist as though he would strike him, and spoke twice as loudly and thrice as harshly, "Have I?"

"Perfectly clear, sir," Robert responded, barely audible.

Robert watched as Scrooge meticulously rolled the paper containing his confession into a small tube. He then retrieved his walking cane and proceeded to unscrew the silver ornamental grip, exposing a hollow compartment in the shaft, into which he slid the paper roll. By this, Scrooge showed Robert that his confession would always be near, as a constant reminder of his crime.

"And forthwith," Marley added, "your pay is reduced to ten shillings a week, which is more than a thief such as yourself deserves!"

Humiliated, bruised, and broken, Robert returned to his office duties. He took solace in his thoughts, as he rationalized the events of the day that were in his favor. *Emily is right, I no longer carry the burden of guilt for my earlier transgression. I am earning ten shillings a week, which I was not earning two weeks ago. And most importantly, I have the love and respect of the woman who will soon become my bride.*

Scrooge was pleased with himself, as well. After feeling resentful for having capitulated to Marley for hiring Robert as an employee, he now felt he had been vindicated for challenging the notion of hiring the clerk in the first place. Besides, Robert's confession of an obviously minor infraction had just saved the business five shillings a week.

That evening, Robert went to the home of Emily's mother and explained to Emily that he had confessed his crime to Scrooge and Marley.

"And have they forgiven you?"

"I don't believe either man knows the meaning of forgiveness, but in their own way, yes. I believe I have been forgiven. Their solution to right my mistake was to reduce my pay to ten shillings."

Emily did not gasp or show anger at the callousness of his employers. She merely took his hand in hers and said, "Today you proved that your love for me is greater than money. Mr. Cratchit, I am ready to become your wife, to have and to hold, until death do us part."

"Even though I am poor?" Robert questioned.

With tender conviction, Emily replied, "I love you *because* you are poor. Your eyes are for me and me alone. I could not be your wife if I had to share you with a golden idol."

The ceremony, held a week later, was a simple one, performed on the front steps of the church where they'd first met. Emily moved into Robert's home, which they shared with his mother. She quickly found work as a cook in a local kitchen, where she earned five shillings a week.

Robert stood near a just lit lamp post, as dusk consumed the shadows surrounding the busy street corner. Peering through the pedestrians, he found the man approaching, for whom he had waited nearly an hour. "Mr. McFadden, sir?"

The tall, well-dressed man turned toward the voice that called his name, and immediately broke into a jovial smile. "Robert, my boy!" he exclaimed, reaching out both hands to shake Robert's right hand. "What brings you out on a muggy night like this?"

"I wonder if I might have a moment of your time, sir, if it's convenient?"

"Quite convenient and quite welcome, sir." Mr. McFadden noticed some empty tables and chairs outside a nearby pub. "Come, my boy. I'll buy us a pint where we can sit, while you tell me what's on your mind." Once the two men walked over and sat down in front of the pub, Mr. McFadden caught the attention of a waiter cleaning the adjacent table and raised two fingers. The waiter nodded, turned and went inside to draw two pints of ale.

"Thank you, kind sir, for the drink and for your time," Robert began. "There is a couple I have come to know, who have one child, a daughter, who is likely dying. Her parents are distraught."

Robert continued to pour out the sad tale of the couple who had spent all they could, and sold all they had to care for their daughter, but who knew the struggle to save her would end soon. Robert knew the young couple's situation, as well as the plans of his ruthless employers. By week's end, they would be evicted; homeless and jobless.

Without a word, Mr. McFadden reached into his vest pocket and pulled out two pounds to place in his friend's hands. "Take this Robert. Pay their rent and help them bury their daughter when the time comes. As usual, please tell them nothing about me; but instead, have the young man come see me when all is said and done, and I will hire him and pay him well to work in my warehouse."

"Oh my gracious! Thank you, sir! Thank you, indeed. I dare not think about the fate of those you have helped, but for your generosity."

Mr. McFadden smiled, closed his eyes for a moment, and replied, "Strange, I was thinking the same thought of you, sir. I dare not think about the fate of so many, had you looked the other way when they needed you the most."

The two friends toasted to each other's health, before Mr. McFadden posed a question of his own. "Robert, I have known you for nearly five years, and in all that time, I have never known you to seek to improve your own situation. Still, I am compelled to ask this of you: would you consider leaving Scrooge and Marley to come work for me?"

Mr. McFadden's offer was genuine and sincere. He had come to love Robert as a son, and could find no other in all of London who had the integrity and loyalty he saw in his young prodigy. Besides his obvious admiration, he knew Robert to be quite a talented clerk who was worth many times the salary he received from Scrooge and Marley.

"I cannot, sir, but thank you all the same," responded Robert after only a moment's thought. Bound now to Scrooge and Marley by the confession of a childhood transgression, he was more a servant to his employers than ever before. Even more so, he still carried the burden of his father's arrest and eventual death, brought on by the ripple of the crime he committed all those years ago.

"But why, Mr. Cratchit? Why would you choose to live in poverty at the wrong end of a tyrant's whip? You know you could do better for yourself and your growing family, if you were to leave Scrooge and Marley."

Robert did not wish to tell his friend and mentor about the debt still owed to Scrooge and Marley, nor the confession Scrooge held over his head, nor the threat of imprisonment and eviction for his family. Instead, he replied with the wisdom of a man fifty years his senior. "I dare say your offer is most generous and more than tempting. Please understand, Mr. McFadden, so long as I labor under Scrooge and Marley, I am in a position to help some of their clients. Not all of them, mind you, but some. I pray I can help those who are most needy. Without providence, and the generosity of such good men as yourself, children will surely go hungry and families homeless. I do not profess to be their savior, merely the *instrument* of their savior."

Mr. McFadden shook his head in amazement at this young man. Spellbound, he could only say, "Bravo, sir. Bravo."

Chapter 9

Looking around the kitchen where she worked, Emily let out a satisfied sigh as she gently pushed back a long, sweaty lock of curly brown hair from her face. All the meals had been prepared and the kitchen was neat and tidy. Today had been another tiring day at work for the young Mrs. Cratchit. On this day, as with every day after work, she gathered her belongings, locked the door behind her and hurried vigilantly through the busy streets of London, dodging fellow pedestrians and perilous encounters with horse drawn carriages before finally arriving home.

"Hello, anyone here?" Emily softly called out, but there was only an eerie silence in the house contrasted by the racket coming from the street outside. "Ahh, a quiet moment," she smiled to herself as she rested her achy back by sitting at the table and lowering her head to her folded arms.

Becky is at the market and Robert is still at work Emily reasoned as she shifted around the hard wooden chair to find a comfortable position. *Today I will tell Robert for sure,* the thought of which transformed the numbing exhaustion she had been experiencing for the last few weeks into tingles of excitement throughout her petite body.

Emily savored the calm of the moment as she rested, and her consciousness drifted in and out of delightfully vivid daydreams of her future with the man she loved. But her euphoria was short lived when unexpectedly she felt a soft, warm kiss on the side of her neck. With a startled squeal, she hastily spun around in the chair, losing her balance.

"Oh dear!" gasped Robert as he seized Emily's arm, preventing her from toppling to the floor, "I didn't mean to frighten you, my love."

Perched on the front end of the chair and staring at the floor, the dazed wife slowly recovered her senses, "Oh, Robert, it's quite all right."

Robert gently released her arm and knelt beside the chair. As if by instinct, Emily looked up as he took her hand in his, and for a brief moment they silently looked into each other's eyes.

"Robert, I need to talk with you about something," Emily began, knowing the time had finally come.

"Yes my love, what's on your mind?"

Pausing for her response, Robert noted what appeared to be a subtle transformation in Emily's appearance. Her skin seemed to glow beautifully, softening the already delicate features of her face, and her bright blue eyes were more sparkly than usual. Softly she whispered, "I think I'm pregnant, Robert,".

Robert's expressive grin dropped as he doubted his hearing. "You—you—what?"

Smiling sweetly, Emily nodded and softly expressed, "Yes my dear, we're going to have a baby."

"Bless my soul!" Robert cried out, throwing his arms around his wife and hugging her, "I'm going to be a father. I have always wanted to be a father, now I am a father!"

Suddenly the front door opened and Becky stepped in, carrying bags of turnips, carrots and potatoes on one arm and some meat bones wrapped in butcher paper under the other arm. "Goodness, this is heavy," she panted as she pushed the door closed with her foot.

"Let us help you," Emily offered, but the couple hugged each other still more lovingly.

"Dears, this is heavy," Becky reminded them a little louder this time.

The loving couple quickly broke their embrace and hurried to her rescue.

After carting the awkward bags to the kitchen table, Emily and Robert began to whisper and giggle. "All right, what has the two of you acting like a couple of lovesick birds?" Becky inquired with a smirk.

Robert put his arm around Emily as they approached his mother. "You're going to be a grandmum," he announced with a broad grin.

Becky's eyes grew wide as she dropped two potatoes to the floor, "I can't believe it. I am going to be a grandmum? Oh how wonderful!"

In their euphoric moment, they exchanged excited hugs and kisses. Becky began humming joyous music as she removed the food from the bags. At that moment she paused and glanced toward the ceiling, "I know just who to use as the midwife." Setting down a bunch of carrots, she turned to the couple and continued, "Her name is Belle. She's a lovely woman who runs a home for women and has delivered countless babies."

Robert and Emily looked at each other and then smiled at her. "That would be splendid, Mother," Robert replied.

"Very well then," Becky confirmed, "I will go see Belle tomorrow."

Fifteen months after the wedding, Emily went into labor with their first child. Becky, and Emily's mother, Martha, each took their turn sitting with Emily, as the young woman's contractions increased. When his mother told him the time was near, Robert ran to fetch the midwife. Upon Belle's arrival, the three women saw to Emily's needs with a sense of calm, yet deliberate expertise, born of experience. As Robert nervously paced in the other room, he continued praying, listening all the while to his wife's cries with each contraction.

Without warning, the front door flung open, causing the anxious father-to-be to step backwards, almost losing his balance. Focusing his eyes, he squinted at the small silhouette standing in the doorway.

"Lizzy, it's you!" Robert sang out as he quickly hurried to embrace his sister.

Returning the hug, she softly kissed her brother on the cheek and followed him into the room.

"How is she?" Lizzy inquired with concern.

Robert flashed a pained smile, "Our Emily is in the best of hands. Belle, the midwife, is incredible."

Suddenly from across the room they heard more cries and muffled talking from behind the closed door.

Letting out an unsettled sigh, Robert regarded his sister with an apprehensive expression on his face.

"Come, sit with me dear brother. We will wait together," Lizzy gently reassured him as she led him to one of the chairs in the modest room.

Lizzy stayed with her brother, periodically passing hot clean towels into the bedroom in exchange for blood soaked towels, which had served their purpose. As the time for the baby's delivery approached, Robert could hear the midwife's voice over that of his wife's, as she yelled, "*Push, push, push,*" followed by a less strenuous command, "Hold it, love. Stop pushing."

This sequence repeated several times, as Robert found comfort in holding his sister's hands. Their conversation quickly subsided, when the two of them could hear the midwife through the closed door. After a long silence, Robert heard small whimpers, followed immediately by the distinct cries of a baby. His eyes opened wide, as he met Lizzy's excited expression and the two siblings hugged.

"What do you think it is?" Robert asked.

"I think it's a girl. Everyone should have an older sister."

"Everyone should have an older sister who is as loving as mine!" Robert added. "If it *is* a girl, we will name her Martha, after Emily's mother. If it is a boy, we will name him Richard."

Just a minute later, which felt like an hour to Robert, Becky emerged from the room humming a sweet lullaby with a bundle in her arms.

Robert stood slowly, still grasping his sister's hand, as his mother gazed at her son. "Robert, come meet your daughter, Martha."

Lizzy jumped up next to her brother with a quick yelp, thrilled that she had guessed correctly. She struggled to pull her hand free from Robert's grasp as he stood frozen in time, looking at a rolled blanket in his mother's arms, trying desperately to process the idea that in there, she held a baby—*his* baby.

"Well, get on with you," Lizzy encouraged, with a slight shove to his back. "Martha wants to meet her father."

Robert's feet finally carried him to his mother and daughter. "Oh, my heavens," he whispered, pulling back the blanket to reveal two closed eyes and a tiny nose.

"Emily?" Robert inquired of his mother.

"She's doing fine, Robert," Becky said, in a comforting voice he loved so well. "You can't go in yet, because the midwife has to deliver the after-birth; but after that, you can take your daughter to her."

Lizzy hugged her brother from behind, sharing in his joy and relishing in his euphoria. She guided her brother back to his chair, so he could sit, before Becky handed the baby to him. Robert looked at his mother and sister, now standing before him, speaking as tears streamed down his cheeks and onto Martha's blanket. "I am so *very* happy."

Lizzy asked the new father, "Do you remember when we lived in Bristol, and I asked father one day what God looked like?"

Robert couldn't take his eyes away from the bundle in his arms, but smiled at the memory, "Yes, I remember."

"You said God is an old man with a long white beard and wears a white robe, and I said God is a giant."

Lizzy looked at her mother who smiled with a nod, encouraging her to continue with her story. "I will always remember what father did. Instead of telling us who was right, he told us he had to make a coal run to the Port of Bristol and that we should ride along.

"Um hm," Robert agreed as he recalled the day. "He stopped the horses near the cliffs to let us watch the tall ships navigate into the harbor. Then he showed us the lighthouse out on the point and said, *to a sailor; that is what God looks like.*"

Lizzy paused to contemplate the day she had relived so many times since then, remembering the spray from the waves crashing rhythmically against the rocky cliffs. Then Lizzy picked up the story, "Without the lighthouse, he told us, ships could not find their way into the harbor at night or in stormy weather. Just as the lighthouse shows the ships the way home, our lighthouse does the same for us."

"Then I remember he said, *you see lad, God is our lighthouse, the light that dispels the darkness from within, to guide us safely home. I tell you, out there past the breakers, ships rest on the bottom in a watery grave, along with the crew who sailed them. Those who did not follow the light met Davey Jones, instead. If you remember nothing else I tell you, remember to seek the light.*"

Robert looked up to her and confirmed, "Yes my dear, I remember it well. Father had a wonderful way of showing instead of telling."

Lizzy continued, "Then he pointed to a field in the valley and asked me if I see God. I told him I did not and he told me to look closer. *Look at the sheep on the hillside and the rows of beans and potatoes beyond the plow.* Then suddenly, I understood what he was teaching us. God is everywhere, satisfying our every need. He guides us when we are lost; he provides food, shelter, even our clothes."

Lizzy paused for just a moment before asking her brother, "Robert, I ask you now, what does God look like?"

Robert squeezed his eyelids to hold back the tears as he realized the answer to her question. He opened his eyes to look into the face of his daughter, "I see God in a newborn baby."

Robert found a renewed zest for life, as he treasured his growing family. Emily left her job to stay home and care for baby Martha, while Robert and Becky continued to work.

Every day, after locking the office door, Robert hurried home. Amongst his family, he found all of the love and comfort he needed following a disappointing and grueling day in the company of Scrooge and Marley. Already feeling better after a tender welcome home kiss from Emily, Robert went to their tiny daughters cradle and bent down to study her perfect face. Little Martha was a beautiful baby, with big, deep brown eyes and thin wisps of golden curls surrounding her tiny face.

"She is beautiful, isn't she?" inquired the proud father, watching as the baby's tiny fingers wrapped around his thumb, "And strong, too. Emily, look at this grip."

Emily chuckled lightly, "You say the same thing every day when you return from work."

"Well, bless me. Emily, look," Robert exclaimed with excitement, "Look, Emily, Martha just smiled at me!"

Shaking her head, Emily giggled softly. She thoroughly enjoyed watching him make such a fuss over the new baby. He had already been a loving husband to her, now he was proving to be a wonderful father to their child.

Barely a month after Martha arrived Lizzy had an announcement of her own. She was expecting her first child, which would be born in about six months. Becky was thrilled to know she herself would be a proud grandmother twice within a year.

Lizzy thoroughly enjoyed watching Martha for Emily from time to time. "It gives me practice," Lizzy said, thoroughly enjoying each and every visit. The two women took great pleasure in each other's company, walking to the markets or strolling through the park on a pleasant spring afternoon, taking turns with the baby.

Lizzy was like a second mother to Martha, caring for her as though she was her own. As the weeks and months passed, Lizzy's baby grew inside her, along with the nervous anticipation of her child's birth. "I am so truly ready for this little fellow to get out of me," Lizzy confessed to Emily, one particularly hot and uncomfortable summer day.

"And what makes you think your baby is a 'fella'?" Emily teased.

"I don't care what 'it' is. I just want him to come out and play with Cousin Martha and stop kicking my backbone!"

Lizzy went into labor on a Sunday afternoon. Robert and Aaron stayed in the kitchen waiting for the news of the blessed event. Becky, Emily and Belle the midwife tended to Lizzy, while Robert tried his best to calm the nerves of his brother-in-law. Baby Martha crawled about the kitchen, distracting the nervous men from watching the clock.

Afternoon turned to dusk, as time slowed the events that followed. Emily passed the news to Robert that the baby was breech, who in turn translated the news for Aaron: "She's doing fine. Emily said it's taking a little longer than usual, because they are trying to turn the baby."

Dusk turned to night and darkness to dawn. Lizzy's screams stopped around midnight, but still nary the sound of a baby's cry. It was Emily who first appeared in the morning's light, carrying a baby wrapped tightly in a blanket. "Aaron, come meet your son," she whispered.

Aaron smiled, as he pulled the blanket from the baby's face enough to see a wrinkled, sleeping little doll. While gently touching the lips of his son, he looked to Emily and asked, "Liz? How is she?"

Emily never took her sight off of the baby to respond, "Go to her, Aaron."

A cold chill hit both Aaron and Robert when they heard the tone in Emily's voice. Aaron ran to his wife's bedside. Robert stood by Emily to hear the prognosis, but Emily could only shake her head and look at Robert with the tears she'd held back for Aaron's sake.

That morning, the entire family remained together, and for the most part, relatively quiet, each caught up in his or her own shock, grief and sense of loss. Emily cared for the baby, nursing him with the milk Lizzy's baby now shared with baby Martha.

Just minutes after the midwife left, neighbors began entering the home to share their grief and comfort the Cratchits and Aaron. Women brought candles to place around the room where Elizabeth Madison lay. Others brought clean sheets to wrap her body, replacing the blood soaked bedding. One kind lady took Martha to her home for a nap, while others brought food for the family, none of whom had eaten for a day.

To Robert, the morning was surreal. Exhaustion from a lack of sleep and food, paired with the shock of his older sister's death, made the horrific event seem like a bad dream. To him, those who entered the small flat and seemed to leave just as quickly appeared to be walking through a fog.

After the noon hour, a tall, lanky undertaker dressed in black tails followed a heavyset woman, who had all but taken charge of the day, into the flat. After cordially offering condolences to Robert and Emily, he entered the room where Becky and Aaron sat near Lizzy's side, so as to prepare the body for burial. He tied a strip of linen around her head and under her chin, in order to hold her mouth closed. After gluing her eyelids closed, he then painted her lips with a red dye.

"I will be back tomorrow with her casket, my dear," the undertaker informed Becky in his very practiced, sympathetic voice. "I will visit your minister this afternoon to schedule the burial and service."

"Thank you, sir," Aaron politely replied.

Before leaving the grieving pair alone with their lost love, the undertaker looked back at the body and mumbled, "So sad to lose one so young." Addressing Becky one last time, he added, "Keep the candles burning, Mrs. Cratchit. It will help mask any unpleasant odors."

Sitting on a wooden stool near the front door, Robert listened attentively, as Emily explained the events of the birth. "It was just too much for her body to stand," she began, still bowled over by the tragedy herself. "Lizzy fought hard to the end. She kept telling us to save her baby, almost as though she knew all along she would not survive herself. And Belle, oh, Robert, the midwife! What she did was an absolute miracle."

"What was it, Em'?"

"When the baby was born, Becky and I looked at each other. We thought for certain he was dead. His entire body was blue and motionless. But that woman, she pulled fluid from his mouth and lungs with her own mouth—then, she flipped him over and pushed on his back. After a few times of doing this and telling him to live, he coughed and sucked in a breath of air on his own. In less than a minute, he was pink and lively. And Robert, the best part of all was that Lizzy heard him. She was unconscious, but when the baby let out his first cry, I'm telling you, your sister smiled."

"She fought to her dying breath to give him life," Robert added.

"Yes, my love," Emily agreed. Then, looking at the baby in her arms, "And now, she lives in him."

It was afternoon before Aaron left the bedside of his departed beloved. Robert stood to give Aaron the seat next to Emily and his son. Becky stayed by her daughter's side, until she had no more tears to give.

"Will you keep him with you until I can care for him?" Aaron asked of Emily, looking at Robert, as well.

"We will," Emily answered immediately. "I will be his wet nurse."

"Absolutely," Robert confirmed.

"Thank you both," Aaron weakly replied. "Mostly, I would like to thank little Martha."

"Why Martha?" Robert inquired.

Aaron managed an innocent smile before explaining, "The time Lizzy spent with you these last few months was so precious to her. Every evening, she would tell me how much she loved caring for Martha, as it helped her experience the joy of motherhood. I am grateful to Martha for giving that gift to Lizzy."

Robert knew Scrooge and Marley would be displeased that he failed to show for work on the previous day (even though it was to mourn the loss of his sister with his family); so Tuesday, he was in the office early, before either of his employers, catching up on the work that was stacked high on his desk, trying hard to write through the tears of a broken heart.

"There you are, you worthless beggar!" Scrooge exclaimed, even before slamming the door behind him. "I assume you found something more important than your position here to occupy your time yesterday?"

Robert stood immediately when Scrooge entered, in order to apologize and explain what had happened, "I am sorry, sir. Please excuse my absence yesterday. I will work this day until I am caught up, I promise. I had a family tragedy to deal with yesterday, which prevented me from being here, sir. It won't happen again."

Scrooge brushed by Robert on the way to his own desk, prepared to rebut any and all excuses that Robert could produce for staying home from work. "Indeed, sir! And just what crisis do you consider more important than earning a day's wages?"

Robert rarely spoke of his family or home life to either Scrooge or Marley, mostly because neither man ever expressed an interest in him personally; but the circumstances of the missed day obviously demanded explanation. "It was my sister, sir. My only sibling you see. She died yesterday, giving birth to her son."

Scrooge stopped dead in his tracks, with his back still toward Robert, before approaching his chair. Robert's words brought back the terrible memory of his own sister, who died under similar circumstances. He sat slowly in his chair, strangely silent. When he saw Robert standing with his head bowed, he responded in an uncharacteristically subdued voice. "I'm sorry to hear that, Mr.

Cratchit. Um, you, you get back to work. We will speak of this no more." Scrooge looked down at his desk, for fear of showing an emotion—not for Robert or his sister Lizzy, but for Fan, the sister whom he once loved.

A week after Lizzy was buried, Aaron called upon the Cratchits. Emily and Becky both hugged him and Robert offered him a cup of tea. Emily placed his son in his arms and watched, as father and son bonded for the first time. He sat in the rocking chair, looking intently at his son's face, searching for the spirit of the woman he loved.

Aaron broke the tension in the room with his first announcement. "Lizzy told me if we had a boy, she wanted to name him after her father. So, I would like you all to meet Peter."

The two women gasped—and in moments, tears streamed down Becky's face.

"Well now," Robert began. "I do say that Peter is a wonderful name for such a handsome boy." Then, leaning forward to address the baby directly, he spoke proudly, "I'm pleased to meet you, Master Peter."

"What a wonderful gift," Becky added.

Emily stood and triumphantly announced to the room, as though introducing the king himself, "Master Peter Madison."

Aaron, too, stood and handed the sleeping baby to Becky, saying, "That's the other reason I'm here." He beckoned Robert and Emily to sit around the eating table with him.

"What is it, Aaron?" Emily inquired.

Aaron took a deep breath, as he prepared to say the words he had rehearsed for several nights. "I cannot care for a child *and* work. My mother has passed, and without my Liz, I have no one to care for a baby. With a heavy heart, I am asking if you will consider raising Peter as your own. I know I am asking the world of you, but will you agree to be Peter's mother and father?"

Aaron looked into the stunned eyes of his brother-in-law and sister-in-law and waited. Becky somehow knew this day would come, sooner or later; but Robert and Emily were not prepared for such a request. A long, weighty moment ticked by without a sound from either Robert or Emily. To break the silence, Aaron offered, "If you need time to-..."

Quickly, Emily interrupted. "I will!" Realizing she had just made a major commitment without consulting her husband in private, she looked to Robert.

He was actually so pleased with his wife's enthusiasm; he too realized he could accept the offer. Speaking from his love for the woman who just agreed to raise his sister's child as her own, Robert chimed in, "We will."

Becky, watching and listening from across the room, pulled Peter to her lips and kissed him on his forehead.

As he looked around the room, Aaron smiled with both a sense of relief and heartfelt joy, pleased at the love he knew flourished in the Cratchit home,."Thank you two so very much. You are the greatest gift I can give my son, and I know that Lizzy is now happy and at peace."

Reaching across the table, the gladdened, yet still grieving widower took one each of Emily's and Robert's hands. They, in turn, held hands to complete the circle. Aaron began to speak solemnly, "It is my wish, and that of my beloved Liz, that you two shall be Peter's mother and father. Becky is Peter's grandmother— this much is certain. But I must hear the words from each of you."

Robert smiled as he looked at Emily and then back to Aaron. "I am Peter's father."

Without hesitation, Emily added, "And I am Peter's mother."

Then Aaron responded with a joyous smile. "And I am the proud uncle of Martha and Peter Cratchit."

The following evening, Robert went to the church where he and Emily, as well as Aaron and Lizzy, were wed, to record the birth of Peter Cratchit.

Chapter 10

Somehow, through the perpetual support of his growing family, Robert managed to continue to find a means to help those in need. Every pence he earned went to the welfare of his *own* family, but his time was another matter. When need presented itself to him, Robert would seek the aid of his ever expanding list of friends and associates for small donations, each of which would have a large impact on a destitute soul or family.

Even those who were not directly indebted to Scrooge and Marley would seek Robert's attention. More and more frequently, a downtrodden man would approach Robert and humbly ask him for assistance. "Pardon me, sir, but I am told you have a kind heart and the means to help a man and his family who are down on their luck."

However, besides the growing list of poor and hungry who came to Robert for help, the list also grew of those who came to him wishing to serve. "Pardon me, sir, but an associate of mine informed me you are a man of character who could make use of charitable resources, while maintaining anonymity."

Many of London's elite and wealthy desired to help those who were less fortunate, but dared not give money to any one man, for fear of being swarmed by hundreds more just like him. Robert, therefore, found himself in the unique position of providing a service to those in need, as well as those with means. By establishing and maintaining a reputation as a man who would protect the identity of the donor, and who was widely known as an honest man who would not pocket the donations for his own benefit, Robert established himself as a trustworthy servant of all.

The third Cratchit child, Belinda, was born on a brisk fall day, bringing warmth to the growing Cratchit family. Unfortunately, as every Londoner knew, chilly fall nights signaled the city's rats to seek refuge in warm homes.

"Where's my 'rat stick'?" Becky asked herself, loudly enough so every human and vermin in the room knew she was on the hunt.

Robert watched his mother pull her arm-sized club from behind the cupboard, and listened as she began a conversation with a rat she was certain could hear her. "Where are you, you filthy rat?" Becky started unloading dishes and food from the cabinet, while continuing to chastise the unwanted guest, "Eat a hole in my flour bag, will you? I'll give you a taste of my *stick* to eat on, I will!"

Belinda twitched in her mother's arms at the sudden sound of Becky's rat stick. First, it hit the back of the cabinet, followed just a second later by an equally startling smack of the stick on the wood floor.

Robert grinned as he reminded Emily, "No rat stands a chance against my mother's rat stick."

"Disgusting creature!" Becky declared, as she carried the dead rat by the very tip of its tail, through the back door to toss it on the garbage pile in the alley. On her way back in the house, she felt a tiny, yet sharp bite on her hand. A single flea had jumped from the rat onto her, as she'd carried the dead animal from her home. Within a few days, her body began to show signs she'd been infected with typhus fever.

Without knowing the extent of her illness, Robert and Emily simply took turns caring for her. The fever persisted, though, raging on for over a week. Neighbors and friends stopped at the Cratchit home to check on Becky. Some brought homemade remedies, other's came to take their leave of the woman so many admired. With every visitor came a cure.

"You just have to let the fever run it's coarse."

"Keep feeding her my chicken soup. I have strong herbs that will burn out the fever."

"Hang garlic above her bed and burn dried basil in her room twice a day.

Emily knew when she married Robert that he loved his mother with all of his heart. She also knew that Robert's love for *her* was just as strong, matched only by the love he had for his children. Becky and Emily would speak often about the man they loved and shared. There was no jealousy between them. To the contrary, the feelings between everyone in the Cratchit household were fueled by the passion they shared for Robert.

While sitting together in a dimly lit room at the end of one day, Emily was the first to utter the words that no one wanted to hear. "Robert, I fear she is dying." Robert stopped his chair from rocking for only an instant, before resuming the rocking motion. He continued gazing intently into the coal-burning fire.

Without responding or even acknowledging her statement, Robert closed his eyes and entered into a silent prayer:

> *Father in Heaven, I humbly beseech Thee to hear the prayer of this, Thy servant. I pray that Thou wouldst spare the life of Becky Cratchit, healing her from the fever that plagues her frail body.*

Over and over, Robert prayed his prayer. Into the sleepless night, he stared at a ceiling that failed to reveal the answers to his questions. *How cruel this world seems,* he thought, *when disease and disorder can strike without regard to innocence or purity of heart.*

The next morning was Sunday—a day without Scrooge and Marley—and on this Sunday, Robert had already planned, it was to be a day without church. Robert woke and quickly dressed, ate some bread with butter from the previous night's meal, and entered the room where his mother lay dying.

Emily was already by his mother's side, cooling her fever with a damp cloth. Looking into her husband's eyes, no words were spoken or needed, as the couple saw the anguish in each other's faces.

"Get some rest, my dear," Robert whispered to his wife. "I'll sit with her, now."

Emily smiled, although somewhat weakly, relinquishing the bedside chair to her husband. Becky's eyes appeared to be sinking away, circled by dark rings. Dehydration was taking a toll on her organs, but her mind was still sharp.

"Mother," Robert beckoned, once he was alone with her. Becky opened her eyes and smiled at the son she cherished. "Mother, can you drink some water for me?"

"I can't, my love."

Robert held one of his mother's hands between both of his, as tears streamed down his cheeks, "Mother, I can't let you die!"

Becky squeezed his hand in response, "That's the wonderful part, Robert. You don't have to. God will let me die, not you."

"What kind of God would take-…"

Becky interrupted him mid-sentence. "The kind of God who gave me two beautiful children. The kind of God who gave you a beautiful family, with a new baby I might add. The kind of God who saves us from our suffering and brings us home to His Kingdom when we are ready."

Robert shook his head in disagreement, "No Mother, no! You can fight this. You are a strong woman and you will beat this cursed fever!"

Wishing to give her son the strength of mind he would need in the days ahead, Becky continued, "Imagine my dear, you had a favorite overcoat you wore day and night. And no matter how worn and tattered that overcoat became, you refused to take it off. This overcoat is what defines you. It is what you see when you look at your reflection. You have never known life without your overcoat and you can't imagine living without it. Now, imagine your overcoat gets so tattered that it no longer keeps you warm or dry. Finally, you realize your overcoat is a nuisance. You suddenly get the strength to take the coat off and drop it to the ground. When you look at your old torn and ragged overcoat lying in a heap on the ground, you realize it serves you no purpose and you don't know why you wore it as long as you did! Without the burden of wearing that old overcoat all the time, you are *free*. You feel lighter. You feel happier. You even look better!"

"Mother, I don't-..."

"Robert, don't you see? My overcoat is weighing me down. I am ready to take it off. It served me well my whole life, but now I need to be *free*."

Two days later, near the hour of ten at night, Robert, Emily, and the minister from their church held hands and prayed next to Becky's bed, as she took rapid, short breaths. Her eyes opened for the first time since that morning, but they did not address anyone in the room. As she followed a light only she could see to the top of the wall, she uttered her last words. "Peter? It's so *beautiful*."

As the minister closed her eyes, Robert embraced his wife, while tears filled his eyes and streamed down his cheeks. With a quiet whisper, respectful of the moment, he asked Emily, "Why was she asking for Peter?"

Emily lifted her head to explain. "Not our son Peter, my love. She saw your father, Peter. He came to show her the way home."

The next morning, exhausted, but strangely at peace, Robert went to work—because he knew not going to work, this time, was not an option. On this particular trip to the office, though, he carried his mother's only overcoat and wrapped it around the shoulders of a homeless woman who sat in a corner to escape the bitter cold near the busy street markets.

The Cratchit family mourned the loss of their beloved mother and grandmother; but more so, they celebrated the life of such a loving and nurturing soul. Becky was buried in the cemetery of the church she had served so faithfully. Friends and family surrounded the Cratchits, sharing stories of affection and memories of a life that had touched all so truly and deeply.

Chapter 11

Robert knew many of Scrooge and Marley's clients. Through the years, many came to the office monthly to settle debt or pay rent. None were kinder to him than Mr. Lucian Knight, a gracious man who always greeted him with a jovial smile and warm handshake. Mr. Knight was many years senior to Robert, but always treated him with respect and friendliness. Having worked for years in a tobacco warehouse, sorting and grading tobacco, he therefore always had a pouch with him of some of the finest pipe tobacco in London. And while he never had more than the month's rent to his name, Mr. Knight always managed to fill Robert's pipe with enough tobacco for him to enjoy a smoke as he walked home from work.

Emily recognized the smell on his coat and scarf when she greeted him at the door. "Old Mr. Knight paid his rent today, I see," she mentioned, giving her husband a second kiss and a grin.

"If London had more men like Mr. Knight," Robert responded, "this good old city would be a finer place."

Emily enjoyed teasing her husband about his infrequent indulgence. An occasional smoke from his pipe was a rare treat he afforded himself when the opportunity arose. But more than that, she enjoyed the nostalgic feelings she would get when the smell of pipe tobacco took her back to a fond memory of her own childhood—sitting on her father's lap, having the special honor of lighting his pipe. Nestled in her father's arms, she would watch in fascination as the smoke rose in swirling patterns from his favorite rosewood pipe.

When Mr. Knight failed to pay his rent for two months running, Robert became gravely concerned. It was uncharacteristic of the kindly old gentleman to neglect his obligations. Robert noticed the two x-marks next to his name in the office ledger, and he knew Marley was tracking the debt. Further, he knew it was only a matter of a month (or two, at the outside) before Scrooge began legal proceedings against him.

One particular evening, as he so often did, Robert told Emily he would be late getting home from work. Without discussing the details, she knew he would be on a mission to help someone through a rough patch. After the closing of business, Robert paid Lucian Knight a visit, unsure of the conditions he might find. Mr. Knight answered the door and greeted Robert with his warm smile and hearty handshake. "Mr. Knight, I'm concerned about your situation. Did you know you are already two months behind your time?"

Mr. Knight motioned for Robert to come in, and both men sat down at a table in the center of the room. Mrs. Knight walked up behind her husband and put both hands on his shoulders, greeting Robert politely, yet oddly looking beside him, without making eye contact.

Grasping one of his wife's hands in his own, Mr. Knight responded, "I am behind my time, sir, and I am heartily sorry, but I have been reduced to only three days a week at the warehouse. I can barely buy the food for the two of us with what little I earn." Mr. Knight began rubbing his wife's fingers tenderly. "If you are here to evict me, I certainly understand, Mr. Cratchit. I bear you no ill feelings for my own shortcomings."

"Oh no, dear sir, I am not here to evict you or your bride. I am here on my own reconnaissance to see if there is anything I can do to help you keep your home, before my employer takes measures."

"Bless you, sir," Mr. Knight replied with appreciation, "but I dare say I have spent many long evenings pondering the same. I must admit, every passing day brings me closer to defeat."

The two gentlemen talked into the night as friends, searching for an answer to a question that had little chance of resolution. Mr. and Mrs. Knight were barren, thus producing no offspring to care for them as they aged. Without being told directly, Robert recognized that Mrs. Knight was losing her sight. She felt for furniture as she moved about the room, finding her way as much with her ears, as with what little sight remained. Still, she managed to make three cups of mint tea to enjoy with some pieces of aging bread.

The days stayed light longer on those hot summer nights. As dusk settled in, Robert felt the need to get home to his family. Although Mr. Knight had barely enough to eat from one day to the next, he still insisted on filling Robert's pipe before he left.

After walking Robert to the door, Mr. Knight paused. "Oh, just a moment, Robert." He turned and hastily made his way into a side room, returning just as quickly. "I want you to have this, sir, to remember our friendship," he said, handing a pipe to Robert.

"I cannot accept this most generous offer, sir," Robert replied, studying the rather unique pipe, carved of wood into the head of a man. The carving included a top hat, which was hollowed to hold the tobacco. "This must surely be a family heirloom, which you treasure."

"No, please Robert, take it," Mr. Knight replied, pushing Robert's hands and the pipe away from himself. "This is just something I made to pass the hours."

"You made this yourself? You carved this masterpiece?"

"I did, and it would do my old heart good to know you found pleasure with it."

"Thank you, sir. Thank you kindly. I shall." Robert carried the pipe through the streets, as if it were fragile crystal, all the while studying the intricate carving and attention to detail. Never before had he been given such a remarkable gift. Interestingly enough, by the time he arrived home, he had already devised a plan to keep

Mr. Knight and his wife in their home.

"I'm sorry I am so late, my dears," Robert said to Emily and each of his children, as he strode in through the front door. Carefully placing the pipe on the mantel over the stove, he acted as if he were displaying a most treasured artwork. For the rest of the evening, even after his children had gone to bed, Robert seemed distant, as if he were absorbed in deep thought.

At last, when Robert and Emily were just about to retire themselves, he took the pipe from the mantel and sat beside her, telling her about his evening with Mr. Knight.

When he told her about his walk home from Mr. Knight's, after receiving the gift, he mentioned his wonderful idea to her, one in which he deeply believed. "I think I can sell this."

"Oh no, Robert, you couldn't sell a gift like this. Mr. Knight poured his heart into this pipe, and you said yourself that he wanted it to be yours to keep and enjoy."

"I didn't mean *this* pipe," Robert recanted, as he touched the top hat of the carving. "I simply imagine I could find a fine tobacco shop that would do well to sell pipes that are hand carved pieces of art, such as this. Don't you see? If I can find the right merchant who would pay a fair price, then Mr. Knight could earn the resources he needs to pay his rent with his carvings, and then some."

Waiting to hear Emily's reply, knowing she was by far the most sensible one of the two, Robert looked at her with yearning eyes. Still clutching the pipe, she greeted his eyes with hers and said, "Have I told you lately how much I love you, Mr. Cratchit?"

Robert hugged her and kissed her cheek, knowing he had just received her blessing to help the elderly couple. This would be one of those nights when he could hardly sleep, his mind racing through the details of the days he hoped would follow.

On the very next evening, after the close of business, Robert left the office and headed in the opposite direction of his home. As he neared the financial district near the London Exchange, he entered an upscale tobacco shop. It was obvious to Robert, and the shop owner who watched him enter, that he would never be able to afford the items on display in this rather high-end shop.

The shop owner approached Robert before he could even make his way to the counter, hoping to politely escort the raggedly dressed man out the door before his wealthy clientele caught sight of him. "May I help you, sir? Are you lost?"

"Yes, sir, I was wondering if I might have a moment of your time." Robert pulled the carved pipe from his pocket and presented it to the owner. "Might you consider selling hand carved pipes, such as this one, in your fine establishment?"

The owner took the pipe out of courtesy, but immediately shook his head, saying, "I'm sorry, but I don't sell local crafts. You would do better to stay in the street markets to peddle your goods." Immediately, he handed the pipe back to Robert.

From behind Robert came a voice he recognized as Mr. McFadden's. "Just a moment, Alfred," he said, addressing the shop owner and pretending to not even recognize Robert. "Let me have a look." Robert handed the pipe to Mr. McFadden, who looked back at Robert with a 'mum's the word' expression on his face. "Hand carved, you say?"

"Yes, sir, by an artist from right here in London."

"You know, Alfred, I would be interested in a pipe like this. How much do you want for it?"

The shop owner looked at Robert and then back to Mr. McFadden, saying, "Uh-... well, when my inventory arrives, those will sell for, um, thirty shillings each."

Mr. McFadden studied the pipe more closely,—as if evaluating the talent of the carver—then handed the pipe to the shop owner and said, "Done and done. I will be back next week to purchase my pipe." Then, looking at Robert, he added, "Make sure the artist signs his work. It will give more value to future generations."

Mr. McFadden promptly returned to his shopping. The shop owner, who had no reason to doubt Mr. McFadden's sincerity, having known him for many years as a fine and loyal customer, suddenly treated Robert with the respect he would grant a London art dealer. Within a few sentences and a gentleman's handshake,

Robert had agreed to supply the owner with exclusive rights to the product and no less than one pipe delivered each week. The shop owner, in turn, agreed to buy each pipe for ten shillings, payable upon delivery, with a thirty shilling advance.

Robert did not look at, nor acknowledge, Mr. McFadden as he left the shop. Neither did Mr. McFadden give notice to Robert upon his exit. Both men would have enjoyed nothing more than to greet and share a pint with each other at a local pub that night, but Mr. McFadden knew Robert was on a mission to help someone *and* that he himself had just aided in fulfilling the goal.

Robert had another long walk before reaching Mr. Knight's door for the second night in a row. This visit, however, would be so much more pleasant than the one the night before. When Mr. Knight opened the door, Robert didn't even give him time to express a warm greeting. Instead, he took the pipe and held it right in front of Mr. Knight's face. "How many more of these do you have, and how long does it take you to carve one?"

"I-... I have a few, I suppose," Mr. Knight replied, somewhat shocked by the rather forceful questions from the young man who had always been so soft-spoken and respectful. "And, I suppose it takes me several days to carve one."

"Good! May I come in, sir?"

"Yes, yes, of course, please come in, Robert."

Within minutes, Robert's news and excitement had been effectively conveyed to both Mr. Knight and his wife.

"Ten shillings? Get on with yourself! You must be joshing an old man."

"No, sir, I am in earnest. He will pay you ten shillings. However, I promised him you could carve at least one a week."

"One a week, yes, yes. That is no problem. But I just can't believe it, Robert! Who would want to buy my-..."

"Oh," Robert interrupted, "and see to it you sign each pipe with your mark. After all, you are an artist, now."

"Robert, I just don't know what to say. Does this mean we can keep our home?"

Robert laughed, as his enthusiasm filled the air. "Keep it and then some, I dare say. The shop owner has advanced the payment for your first three pipes!" He showed Mr. Knight the thirty shillings from his pocket. "I will use this to settle things on your behalf with Mr. Scrooge and Mr. Marley."

Mrs. Knight hugged her husband's neck from behind, with tears filling her eyes. "Oh, Lucian, my love." A welling up of deep emotions prevented her from speaking further.

Robert received some truly heartwarming compensation for his good deed, when Mr. Knight replaced his typical handshake with a hug, just as Robert left their home, whispering in his ear, "Thank you, my friend. Thank you."

Chapter 12

A few months passed after the events relating to Mr. Knight before Scrooge laid an envelope bearing the name "Miller" on Cratchit's writing table. Robert didn't even need to ask—he knew the Millers had not paid their mortgage in months, and Marley had begun foreclosure proceedings. Unlike a delinquent renter, a foreclosure was more intrusive, as Scrooge and Marley would seize the property and sufficient personal belongings to compensate the missed payments.

The Miller mortgage was for a small sheep farm south of London. "Take a constable with you, if need be," was all Scrooge said, as he continued past Robert to his own desk.

"Yes, sir, Mr. Scrooge."

"And take a shilling from the cash box for a carriage. You have a three-hour trip before you."

"Thank you kindly, sir." Robert grabbed a shilling from the lock-box, retrieved his hat, and just as he departed the office, said, "Your servant, Mr. Scrooge."

The door nearly closed behind him, before Scrooge could respond with a raised voice, "You'll do well to remember that fact, sir!"

The carriage ride to the Miller farm was long and dusty, but any time Robert could spend hours away from his miserly employers was welcome. The fresh country air cleansed his lungs, while the green meadows carried him back to his childhood years, growing up in Bristol. The sight of a man and young boy quietly fishing at a pond not far off the road retrieved some cherished memories for Robert, of the many lazy Sunday afternoons he'd spent with his father.

As the carriage approached the Miller farmhouse, Robert believed he would find the home deserted. *This will be easy*, Robert thought, imagining himself nailing the notice to the door of an empty house.

The house, fencing, and barnyard were all in disrepair. No sheep, chickens, or animal of any sort were in sight; not even the expected sheepdog. Robert bid the carriage driver to wait for his return, as he approached the front door with hammer and nail in hand.

Upon raising the hammer, Robert stepped back in shock when the door opened and a frail young lady came forward, questioning him with a single word. "Sir?"

Startled by the unexpected occupant, he lowered the hammer and removed his hat. "Oh, madam! Please forgive me. I didn't realize anyone was home. Would you by chance be Mrs. Miller?"

The young lady leaned into the doorway, looking both ways, as if surveying the scene to determine if anyone other than Robert and the carriage driver was about. "I am, sir. And you?"

"I do apologize, my dear. My name is Robert Cratchit. I serve the office of Scrooge and Marley."

"Yes, sir?"

"Is your husband about, Mrs. Miller?"

She took another small step onto the porch and again searched the area with her eyes. Still speaking in a subdued voice, she answered, "I beg your pardon, kind sir, but he will likely be home after dark."

As she stepped into the light, Robert saw that her face was bruised and her left eye was swollen shut. "Oh, my dear, are you alright?"

"Mummy?"

Slowly taking his eyes from the woman's battered face, Robert looked down to see an unkempt little girl pulling on her mother's apron. Returning his attention to Mrs. Miller, he asked, "Did someone hit you?"

She nervously shook her head 'no.'

"Did your husband?"

Again shaking her head 'no,' she cautiously surveyed the road, where Robert's carriage waited.

"Let's sit down and talk," Robert suggested, directing her to a bench on the front porch. As they sat, her daughter stayed close by her side, and Robert began carefully explaining to the young Mrs. Miller that Scrooge and Marley had been holding the mortgage on her farm *and* that her husband was many months behind on their mortgage payments.

"Please understand, sir," she replied, "the farm has failed and my husband has sold everything he could, including the animals. Now, most evenings, he takes what little money he has to the pub."

Robert suddenly regretted passing on Scrooge's suggestion to bring a constable. *This poor lady,* he thought, *and probably her daughter, as well, have obviously been the recipient of her husband's drunken rage.* "I'm truly sorry," he said, "but I must leave this foreclosure notice for your husband."

Her hand trembled as she took the envelope, knowing its contents would indeed invoke his violent wrath.

Staring at her swollen eye, Robert offered her a proposal. "Given your situation, I'd like you to consider accompanying me to London, where I can help you find a safe haven. Please believe me, I know people who can help."

"Thank you kindly, sir—but no, this is our home." Looking down at the envelope in her hand, she corrected herself. "Or at least it *was* our home."

"Please," Robert implored. "It's not safe for you here."

"No, we will be well." Mrs. Miller stared off as she responded, as though trying to believe her own self-deception, while combing her fingers through her daughter's filthy, tangled blonde hair.

The ride back to London was troubling. Robert tried to devise a plan to help Mrs. Miller and her daughter, but nothing seemed plausible. *It would be futile to seek resources to catch up the delinquent mortgage payments. The farm is obviously dead,* he reasoned. *And Mr. Miller will keep drinking and mistreating his family. No, I can't imagine anything would help.*

Hearing himself "giving up" startled Robert, a man who'd helped countless people in similarly improbable situations. He committed, at that moment, to seeing his way through to a satisfying outcome. *Somehow, I will think of something! I must get Mrs. Miller and her daughter away from him. I will talk with Emily tonight. She will know what to do.*

The business of Scrooge and Marley was closed, by the time the carriage returned to London. Robert made his way home and held his wife tightly in a loving hug. Emily knew her husband's heart and asked right off, "Robert? What is it?"

Releasing his grip on his wife, he sat at the table to eat his waiting dinner. "Em, I just don't know what to do. I know how to help someone who wants help, but I don't know how to help someone who needs help, but also refuses."

"What happened today?"

"Well, Mr. Scrooge sent me to serve a foreclosure notice at a small farm south of town, which by the way explains my lateness in returning from work. I'm sorry."

Emily smiled, appreciating how considerate her husband could be, no matter the situation.

Robert continued, "A young man, his wife and child, but I only met the wife and child. I could clearly see severe bruising on her face and hands. She was scared to death to even talk to me. I must confess, Em, there is no denying she is regularly beaten by her wretched husband."

Emily gasped, bringing up her hand to cover her mouth at the grim picture Robert painted.

"Her unwashed, scruffy daughter was terrified into silence. I begged the mother to come with me, but she would not. I am so afraid, my love, that things will only get worse for this poor woman and her little girl."

Tears filled Robert's eyes, as he told his day's story. "Robert," Emily interrupted, "whatever it takes, you must get her and her child away from there. If what she told you is true, her husband is a violent drunk, and when he sees the foreclosure notice, he will blame her, for certain."

"I agree, but how can I get her to leave, when she is so afraid?"

"She fears you because you're a man. Pity she does not know what a gentle, caring man you are. Show her what I already know about you. She will trust you and see you are a living sanctuary."

"Well, the notice was served, so Scrooge will not spend a pence on another trip to the farm. But I believe I could ask Mr. McFadden for a carriage and driver. I'll go after the close of business tomorrow and do all I can to bring her here, to our home. She told me her husband is out drinking most evenings, so I have a good chance to find her home alone." A look of caution swept over his face. "We must be very careful, Em'. Our plan *could* be dangerous."

"That's true, Robert—but if we don't try, if we fail to get her, the danger is even greater."

Sleep did not come easy to Robert that night, despite the long day. If he was, indeed, able to convince Mrs. Miller to return to London with him, there was a very real chance that her husband could track her to the Cratchit home, which would expose his family to an obviously violent man. He continued tossing and turning in bed, pondering what he might do given the various possible scenarios he might end up facing. Just as both his mental and physical exhaustion were bringing him to the brink of a much-needed sleep, the frightening sound of a young girl's cry for help compelled Robert to jump from bed straight into the middle of the darkened room.

Emily continued sleeping soundly, so Robert quickly maneuvered through the darkness to where Martha slept, thinking she may have had a nightmare. However, he found both Martha and Belinda sound asleep, as well. Looking around, he realized the only one stirring in the Cratchit home was he himself.

The rest of the night was predictably restless. Every time sleep would approach, Robert remembered the cry for help that disturbed him so. *Had it been a neighbor calling out*, he thought, *she could still be in dire need of help.* Yet, listen as he might, the one crying out earlier remained silent.

In the light of dawn, Robert told Emily about his sleepless night. "See here, what you heard was probably a nightmare," she replied. "And I can tell you this much is true: you'll do the best you can, Robert Cratchit, and then you must let God take over from there. Now, get yourself dressed and off to work! You have a long day ahead of you."

While walking to work, already exhausted before the day began, he rationalized the long, arduous night and his hearing a scream was caused by his concern for the young woman he had met the previous day. *The haunting cry for help still sends chills through my body, nightmare notwithstanding,* Robert concluded.

"Did you deliver the notice yesterday?" Scrooge asked, as he entered the office.

"I did, sir, to Mrs. Miller. Mr. Miller was not home."

Scrooge paused for a moment to consider the transaction, and then nodded with acceptance. "Good."

Nothing else was said about the Millers, until later that afternoon, when a constable entered the business and looked at Cratchit, who sat nearest the front door. "Mr. Scrooge or Mr. Marley?"

"This way, sir," he gestured, escorting the constable to the room where Scrooge and Marley worked.

Again the constable queried, "Mr. Scrooge?"

"I am, sir. Can I help you?"

The constable laid the foreclosure notice for the Miller farm on his desk. "I believe this is yours, sir. I have just returned from the most gruesome scene. I'm sorry to say the mother and daughter have been killed."

Standing by his desk, Robert could hear the entire conversation. He sat down slowly, before his knees failed him.

"Are you sure of this, sir?" Scrooge questioned. "My clerk delivered this foreclosure only yesterday."

"I am earnest, sir, though I wish I were not. We were summoned to the farm last night by a neighbor who heard screams. We found this notice on Mrs. Miller's chest with a knife through it. The child was on the floor near her mother, dead, as well."

Marley joined the conversation. "And Mr. Miller? Was he about?"

"We believe Mr. Miller killed them both and has fled—but I promise you, sir, we will find him."

"Yes, I'm sure you will," said Scrooge. "Thank you, sir. Thank you for bringing us the news. Good day, sir."

"Good day, and again, I apologize for the situation," replied the constable.

Robert slowly rose from his chair, out of respect, as the constable let himself out. Neither man was able to speak even a courteous parting word.

Robert walked to the door of the office where Scrooge and Marley worked, and in his shock, sought comfort in conversation with his employers. "They are dead, Mr. Scrooge? But I just saw them."

"Yes, dead, Mr. Cratchit. What concern is that of yours?"

"Actually," Marley joined in, "this makes our job easier altogether. Foreclosures are slow and costly, but Mr. Miller just handed the farm to us as a gift."

"True," Scrooge added with a grin, "very true, indeed." The business partners reached between their desks to shake hands with a hearty, "Congratulations!"

Robert returned to his desk, still reeling from the shock of the morning news. He bowed his head and whispered, "I'm sorry. I am *so* sorry."

When Robert walked through the front door that evening, he knew his wife had been preparing all day for him to return from the Miller farm, accompanied by a terrified mother and child. She did not know, could not know Mrs. Miller's fate, until he told her. However, Emily knew the plan must have changed as Robert did not arrive by coach. "What has happened, Robert? Where are Mrs. Miller and her daughter?"

He beckoned her to sit with him, as he told her the news. Upon hearing of the two brutal murders, Emily sobbed with tears for the woman and child she had only met through her husband's words. Sometime later, after consoling his wife and her crying had stopped, Robert shared his true sentiments. "I failed, my dear. I failed that dear woman and her child. Why didn't I insist she go with me the first time?"

Emily stood up immediately from the table where they'd been sitting. "Robert, stop! Do *not* pick up this cross. You did everything you could! It just happened, Robert. It just happened."

"The scream, the cry for help I was certain I heard—is it possible what I really heard was Mrs. Miller calling out?"

Emily comforted her husband in his time of distress. She listened, as he talked, reflecting on the horrific life Mrs. Miller must have suffered. When he spoke of the callous words and behavior of Scrooge and Marley, he remembered his shame for being their clerk. "You are not responsible for what others think, say, or do, Robert. Just pray your spirit never succumbs to the black hearts of such odious, despicable men."

The couple talked well into the night, until Robert, drained both physically and emotionally, crawled into bed, hoping for sleep's sweet release.

The sound of a carriage rolling over the cobblestone street, accompanied by the rhythmic steps of a horse, caused Robert to open his eyes, as he watched the dim light from a lantern on the carriage move across his ceiling in the opposite direction. When the sounds from the carriage faded, the light persisted just above the foot of his bed, descending toward the floor as it grew in intensity. Robert propped himself on both elbows, focusing on the brilliance before him. Slowly, a human figure manifested in the midst of the light. As the lucent figure took focus, Robert suddenly realized he was looking at Mrs. Miller. Her face was clean and pure, however, and the previously swollen eye was now open and clear. Her hair emitted a light that radiated in all directions. She said nothing, but looked directly in his eyes, smiling at him with a look of sincere compassion.

Robert remained fixated on the specter before him, unable to speak. Feeling no fear, he watched her look down to her side. Following her lead, Robert saw a second figure of light standing alongside, a child with a glowing light as brilliant as the first. He flinched, when a burst of light from the pair pulsed toward him, engulfing him with the purest feeling of love he had ever experienced. Both figures looked directly into Robert's eyes and smiled one final time, as the light faded to darkness.

Chapter 13

Robert was twenty-four when the fourth Cratchit child, Richard, blessed the growing family. Even though Martha was only six, her "nurturing instincts" were a blessing to her parents, as she mimicked her mother and helped care for baby Richard more as a mother than as a sister. It was two years after Richard's birth that Martha, Peter, Belinda, and Richard welcomed the fifth and final Cratchit child, who they named Timothy.

Timothy seemed like a healthy, happy baby at first; but just days after his birth, Emily realized something was amiss. He could keep very little of her milk down. As his eating disorder persisted, he grew very slowly, remained small for his age, and was slow to start walking. Instead, he sat quietly, watching and learning from those around him.

All of the Cratchits, both big and small, cared for Timothy, often treating him like a china doll, for fear he might break. He seemed listless at times, mostly due to the meager calories he could digest. Still, his fragile, quiet nature made him seem content with his situation. That, with his small stature and gentle demeanor attracted many of the neighborhood women who wanted to hold and nurture him.

As he took his first steps (at nearly the age of two), Robert and Emily noticed he could step flat on his left foot, but tended to walk on the outside of his right foot. The more he grew, the more his foot turned inward. By the time he was three years old, he could only walk with the assistance of walls and furniture for support, often opting to crawl instead.

Old Mr. Evans, a caring neighbor, constructed a crutch for Timothy, or "Tiny Tim" as people began calling him. He customized it for Tiny Tim's size, and wrapped cloth on the armrest to make it more comfortable for him to use. With his wooden crutch always near his side, Tiny Tim felt the freedom of mobility, as he followed his siblings and parents alike. Although he would tire easily, he'd hobble-walk his way around the house and throughout the neighborhood, never once complaining.

Everyone who knew Tiny Tim loved him for his perseverance and sweet disposition. Everyone who watched him was inspired by his determination to be like the other children his age. Even the local bullies took no pleasure in teasing him. He seemed to soften the heart of even the most hardened souls.

Robert carried Tiny Tim on his shoulder when they went about town. Not because he was impatient toward waiting for Tiny Tim to catch up, but because Tim loved being "the tallest person in the crowd," meeting and greeting people at their height. There was no sound in all the world that Robert enjoyed more than Tim's laugh, so he made every shoulder ride a real treat. Tim would giggle persistently when his father would gallop down the street making clip-clop noises, as Tim bounced up and down on his shoulder as if riding on a saddle.

The bond between father and son was strong. Fortunately, there was not a bit of jealousy among the other Cratchit children for their father's attention. To the contrary, they loved Tiny Tim's smile and laughter as much as Robert and Emily did.

One evening, Robert decided to shortcut his way through some alleys in hopes of getting toward his part of town quicker. He had just secured the ten shillings necessary to pay one more month's rent to keep the Wallace family in good standing with Scrooge and Marley. This was the third time he had come to their assistance, but there was no avoiding the situation. Mr. Wallace had a broken leg and would be unable to work his position as a brick layer for at least another month. Besides, they had a daughter who was about Tim's age who occasionally played with his son.

As he walked, Robert heard a swishing sound, like ocean waves crashing on the shore, followed by silence. Standing in a meadow he'd enjoyed as a boy, Robert saw Peter, his father, walking toward him. "Father?"

"It's not time yet, Robert," his father told him, in the gentle voice that comforted him as a child. "There is still so much for you to do. But know this, my son; the love you give will come back to you, just like the ripples in the bucket."

Robert felt a sense of peace and love stir in his soul, stronger even than the feelings he shared with his family. "Father, can I stay here with you?"

Peter turned and grabbed both of Robert's shoulders. He started yelling, as he shook him, "Sir! Sir! Can you hear me? Are you alright? Sir!"

His father's voice changed to that of a stranger's, as the bright meadow faded into the darkness of a back alley. Before him, he could see a man's face slowly coming into focus. Again, he heard the man calling out, "Sir, sir," but now this man was shaking his shoulders where his father had been holding him only moments before.

"What?" Robert heard himself ask. Looking side-to-side, he realized he was sitting on the ground with his back against a brick wall and his hands down at his sides in the wet gutter. He could feel the water of the open sewer beneath him, soaking his pants. "What happened? Where am I?"

The man before him, a kind Samaritan, replied, "I don't know. I was just walking home when I saw you here in the alley. Can you try to stand? This is not a good part of town to loiter, if you get my meaning."

"Yes, yes, I think I can walk. I must have tripped or something."

"Judging by the blood on your head, I would say you hit pretty hard."

Robert felt the swelling knot on the back of his head, and then saw blood on his hand. Suddenly, a cold chill rushed over him, as he reached for the ten shillings in his pocket. "Gone! The money is gone!"

"My goodness, sir, you did not trip! You were robbed!"

"Robbed?"

"Put your arm around my neck and walk with me. I am going to take you to my home and get you fixed up. Maybe not right as rain, but close enough to a sprinkle." A couple of blocks later, Robert and the man were climbing the front steps toward his home.

"Sit here," the kind man instructed, as he escorted Robert to a chair." My wife will get some clean towels and alcohol to dress your wound."

Robert's senses were slowly returning, as the pieces of the night were coming together. "My name is Robert Cratchit, kind sir."

"And I am Fred Holloway. I dare say, Mr. Cratchit, I wish we could have met under better circumstances."

As Mrs. Holloway cleaned the head wound with a towel dipped in whiskey, Robert flinched, as, for the first time, he felt the pain of where he'd been hit.

Robert opened up to Mr. Holloway and his wife, as they sat and talked. Both refused to allow him to leave until they were certain he could walk without incidence. He tried to answer their questions as truthfully as possible, even when asked why he was walking through an alley at night in a part of town with which he was unfamiliar.

"Scrooge? Ebenezer Scrooge of the firm Scrooge and Marley?" Mr. Holloway exclaimed.

"Yes, I say I know of none other by that name," Robert replied, as the conversation suddenly took a sharp turn.

"Why bless my soul! Ebenezer Scrooge is my uncle, my mother's brother, as a matter of fact," Mr. Holloway said, amazed at the coincidence of the situation.

"Strange, I've never heard him mention a nephew, or any family at all, for that matter."

"That fact does not surprise me in the slightest. The old coot has had nothing to do with me my entire life. I say, I have only met the man a few times and those were not pleasant encounters, I must admit. You see, my mother died giving birth to me," Fred explained, "a circumstance for which he has begrudged me my entire life."

"Oh my," Robert responded, as he considered the similar circumstances to the loss of Lizzy. "I too lost my beloved sister during the birth of her son. We brought him into our family and raised him as our own. I can't imagine life now without my son, Peter."

As the evening passed into night, the two men talked as though they were old friends. Fred was embarrassed to hear the sort of man his uncle was, but was equally impressed to know Mr. Cratchit. When Robert explained how he took it upon himself to solicit resources to pay the debts of those at risk of losing their homes from Scrooge and Marley, Fred couldn't wait to help.

"Oh no, sir, I must say you have done more than enough for me already," Robert responded, when Fred offered to make good the stolen ten shillings.

"Please, Mr. Cratchit. Look at this as my way of sticking it to my estranged uncle," Fred implored with a slight grin.

"Yes, please, Mr. Cratchit," Fred's wife chimed in. "Please, for our sake, if not your own."

Mr. Holloway walked Robert halfway home, until he was certain there would be no more problems. Then, the two new friends parted, but not before Fred promised to come visit his uncle and reacquaint himself.

When Robert arrived home, Tiny Tim was asleep on his mother's lap, having conceded to the need for rest. Emily was beside herself with worry. She didn't know whether to hug him or chastise him for being out so late. After hearing his apology, and the horrible story of being knocked unconscious before being robbed, she decided both responses were in order.

"Robert, I wish to high heaven you would look out for yourself with a good deal more sense of safety!" she said, as she wrapped her arms around his neck and held him tightly in a close embrace.

Typical of her husband, he managed to tell the remaining details of the story to her in such a way as to arrive at a most surprising conclusion. *Only Robert Cratchit*, she thought to herself when he reached the end of his tale, *could see the bright side of nearly dying at the hands of robbers.* But as he explained, "I would never have met the nephew of Mr. Scrooge, had it not been for the attack. I don't know how, my dear, but somehow I believe it is important I have met Mr. Holloway. Maybe because of the dream, or I dare say vision, of my father just before we met. Yes, that could be vitally important, I think."

After redressing his wound, the two went to bed for the few hours that remained of the night.

Chapter 14

"Cratchit!" broke the silence of the office, when Scrooge called for his clerk. Robert jumped up, knowing he had only seconds to present himself in front of Scrooge's desk whenever he was called upon.

"Yes, sir, Mr. Scrooge?" was his response, as he came to a sudden halt at his usual spot in front of his employer.

"Take this and serve notice." Scrooge handed him an all-too-familiar notice of eviction. "And make haste. No loitering about with you, am I clear, sir?"

"Yes, sir, right away. Your servant, Mr. Scrooge." Robert turned to make his way.

"Yes, yes, I know you are. You don't have to keep reminding me." He said this, even though Scrooge loved nothing more than to be reminded he had a good and loyal servant.

Robert was fluent with the task of serving eviction notices for Scrooge and Marley. He opened the office's cabinet door to reveal a wall of keys. Each hung on its own nail, and each was tagged with a different address. These were the spare keys to all of the properties owned by Scrooge and Marley. Robert matched the address in the eviction notice to the key labeled as such, and picked up the hammer and a single nail from a wooden box on the bottom of the cabinet. If the resident was not home, or would not answer the door, he would gain entrance with the key and, if necessary, hang the notice on the door with the nail.

When Robert arrived at the home, he knocked several times, but the tenant did not respond. As luck would have it, as was so often the case, the tenant had vacated the premises without informing the landlord. Many of those who knew Scrooge and Marley could not stomach the idea of informing them they were moving from the rented quarters; instead, they would just silently leave.

Robert simply spent a moment or two hammering the notice on the door, as a matter of formality. He then diverted a couple of blocks from his route back to the office, in order to pay a visit to the tobacco shop that sold Mr. Knight's crafts. He entered the shop and was heartily greeted by the owner, Alfred, who had become fond of Robert's good nature. "Mr. Cratchit, good day, sir," came his greeting from behind the counter. Robert often came to the shop to enjoy the fresh scent of fine tobacco, as well as to enjoy hearing the success stories about Mr. Knight's hand carved pipes.

After a friendly conversation and a gentle pat on the back from the shop's proprietor, Robert scurried through the streets to get back to the office, before he would be considered delinquent. Immediately upon entering the office, Robert went directly to the keys cabinet to return the key and hammer to their proper place. "Well?" came the request from behind Scrooge's desk.

"Vacated, sir," was Robert's reply. After years of service, Robert could communicate with Scrooge and Marley with minimal conversation, which was as they preferred it. Scrooge knew that Robert would make the appropriate entries in the ledgers, indicating that the vacated property would now be available for rent. As if on cue, Robert pulled the ledger from the shelf and returned to his desk, where he opened the book and started making his entries.

Robert did not look up from his book, nor did he pause from writing, as the door opened and then slammed shut. He knew by instinct that Marley had returned to the office and was in a dreadful mood. Robert's instinct failed to warn him, though, that he was the source of Marley's anger. Had he known, he would have tried to evade Marley's rage. He flinched as a sudden crack of wood slammed down just in front of him. He watched as the broken half of the wooden cane deflected off of his desk and flew across the room. Looking to his left, he could see the blood already pooling on top of his left hand.

It must have been several seconds before he realized the pain he experienced in his hand. One of the bones that broke actually did him a favor by severing a nerve. He lifted his hand from the desk and watched as his knuckles immediately swelled and discolored—purple and blue—from the broken vessels that were leaking blood, both below and above the skin.

Robert pulled his hand against his chest and cradled it with his right hand, as he looked to see Marley glare at him with pure hatred. "Bloody hell!" Marley screamed, not necessarily at Robert, but just in general.

Scrooge had watched the entire scene unfold from his desk and could not imagine what had his partner so riled. "Jacob!" Scrooge called out, nearly as loud as Marley had just yelled. "What ails you, sir?"

Marley was breathing hard, as if he had just run from the devil himself, pointing with what was left of his broken cane at Robert, "This ungrateful street urchin was just over by the London exchange! I saw him, with my own eyes, coming out of a tobacco shop."

Scrooge looked at Robert, who was now wincing as the pain set in, then back at Marley, "So? And what concern is this of mine, or even yours, for that matter?"

"We lost the bid for the Masson property!" Marley snapped back, waving a document over his head. "Had he been here, instead of running around London like the beggar he is, I could have had him run this bid to the broker's in suitable time."

"But Jacob," Scrooge answered with a condescending voice, "you were supposed to have delivered that bid two days ago. And besides, I sent Robert out to serve a closure."

Marley attempted to salvage what dignity he had left. "I know I was, but I forgot and just found it in my coat this morning. And besides..." he stopped himself in mid-sentence, looked at Robert and the broken cane still in his hand. "Bloody hell!" he yelled again, as he flung the remnant of the cane across the room and left the office with a slam of the door, just as violently as he had entered.

Scrooge chuckled at his partner's error, but stopped short when he looked at Robert clutching his hand in agony. He watched in silence as his employee tried to keep his blood from spilling on the floor with his shirt. Pointing the feather end of his quill behind him, Scrooge said, "Go out back and clean yourself, Robert. Then, get back to work."

Robert quickly hurried out the back door of the office into the alley. He dropped to his knees next to the gutter, where water flowed continuously, carrying waste water toward the underground sewers. The smells of the open sewer and pain in his hand caused him to suddenly vomit. Feeling faint, he pulled off his undershirt and dipped it in the cool water to wipe the beads of sweat from his face. He then held the shirt with his good hand and also with his teeth, and proceeded to tear it into strips. With these, he bandaged and wrapped his left hand, which continued to swell. Staring down at his hand, discolored and disfigured, he hesitated for a moment, remembering how he used this very hand to steal ten shillings from Scrooge's desk and clutch it through the streets of London.

The blood pool under the skin covered the entire back of his hand and flowed into his wrist. The bones in his middle and index finger were broken beyond repair. But for now, he stopped the bleeding, wrapped his hand, and returned to work.

It was not unusual for Marley to be out of the office, as he often looked for opportunities to improve the company's holdings, usually by taking advantage of businesses that were in a desperate situation. Still, this time was somewhat different, as Marley now stayed away from the office to dodge confronting Robert Cratchit. When he did return, the two men avoided eye contact—Marley, out of shame for losing his temper and crippling the hand of his clerk, and Robert, for fear of crossing his employer and, however unintentionally, inviting another devastating strike.

Robert had learned to expect the unexpected from Scrooge and Marley. So it was true to nature, during a rare moment while Scrooge was out of the office, when Marley finally addressed him in an unexpected manner. "Er, uh, listen, Robert. I feel that I must beg your pardon for my behavior the other day. I was not in control of my faculties."

"No sir, it is I who should apologize. I realize I should not have been neglecting my position by entering the tobacco-…"

Marley raised his hand to hush Robert in mid-sentence, "Robert, please, let me. There was no excuse for what I, that is to say—I have thought much about this for the last two nights. I know this will not heal your hand, and God knows that I would give you my own hand, if I could."

Robert was struck with awe, as he listened to Mr. Marley. Neither Marley nor Scrooge had ever spoken to him so compassionately before. In fact, he could not remember a single moment when he had been allowed to feel like a viable human in the office of Scrooge and Marley.

Marley continued. "I know your family is growing, sir. I would like to make amends to you by offering you and your family the vacant rental upstairs above your current flat. It has three rooms, besides the common room."

Robert smiled for the first time in days. "Bless my soul, kind sir! What a generous offer. But I could not afford such a place as-…"

"Sir," Marley interrupted again, "I am sincere. The arrangements are as before. Your rent is part of our agreement with your employment—and your salary, going forward, is *now* fifteen shillings a week. Consider this your long overdue raise."

Marley couldn't help smiling at Robert, as he saw his clerk's face light up. In practice, the rental would normally be four shillings more a month than his current accommodations; so it was not a big impact on the business, certainly not as much as Robert was making it out to be.

Robert held his enthusiasm for another moment, when he asked with apprehension, "But, sir, what about Mr. Scrooge? Will he-..."

"I will handle my partner and my business, sir. You just get the key from the cabinet and move your family into your new home after the close of business tonight."

"I shall, I shall, and thank you most kindly, sir. This is a most unexpected surprise." Robert pictured the expression on his family's faces when he would share the news with them.

Robert's employers never struck him again. They both knew the incident with the cane had gone too far. There was also the constant reminder when they would watch Robert work with his two damaged fingers, unable to move or clasp, as the bones had fused into a permanent position. What they *didn't* see was the pain that was always present in his hand.

Chapter 15

Neither Marley nor Scrooge ever married or had children of their own. The business was their mistress and she was never satisfied. Robert had become the son who Scrooge or Marley never had, even though he was usually treated more like their dog.

As the days and weeks passed, Scrooge began to notice that Marley was softening in his treatment of their clerk. "Jacob," Scrooge began in a private conversation, "if you don't stop coddling Cratchit, he will begin taking advantage of you. Remember who the master is, and who is the clerk."

"I am not coddling him," Marley responded defensively. "I merely treat him with a teaspoon of dignity." The two men argued the matter for the next half hour. Marley capitulated to a degree, knowing Scrooge would crack down harder on Cratchit, if he believed Marley to be easing back. In front of Scrooge, Marley maintained his gruff nature; but in private, it was not unusual for Marley to address Robert with a kind word.

The more pleasant atmosphere around the office was short-lived. By November, Marley was bedridden more days than he worked. Marley's charwoman called on a doctor, overruling her employer's objections, who was obviously angry about the inevitable expense. The doctor did little more than advise her to try to find some food he could keep down. And while the good doctor did not understand the cause of the man's failing health, he *did* recognize a dying man when he saw one. "Keep his lips wet and let him have all the whiskey he wants for the pain," he told the charwoman outside of Marley's range of hearing. "He won't be leaving this room until the undertaker carries him out."

Scrooge never visited Marley. Instead, he was somewhat perturbed with Marley for leaving him with all of the work involved in keeping the business running. Robert, however, visited Marley several days a week after work. Marley would pretend to detest the visits, but in truth appreciated the company, none the less.

Even though Marley was never a religious man, he was a God-fearing man. Thus, he rarely protested when Robert would pull up a chair next to his bedside and read aloud, select passages from the Bible. Marley knew he was dying, even though no one had told him as much. Over the course of the following days and weeks, Marley realized that the clerk, who he had treated so horribly for the last sixteen years, was in the end, his one true friend. To Scrooge, Marley was merely a means to an end. But to Robert, Marley could tell he meant something more, even if he was a lonely man with little connection to anything or anyone outside of his business.

Robert reflected on his father's words, as he sat by Marley's bed, watching him sleep. He remembered learning about how ripples in the water represent a man's deeds. "Bad deeds ripple out just the same as good deeds," he recalled his father saying. He contemplated all of the lives Marley had touched with his own, and prayed that Marley be spared the pain he had dealt to others.

Near the end, Robert looked down to see Marley's hand move across the bed to embrace his own crippled left hand. He looked up to see that Marley had awoken and opened his eyes, ever so slightly, and with barely a whisper, asked, "Robert, can you ever forgive me?"

Robert resisted the urge to tell Marley there is nothing to forgive, or that he was talking nonsense, because he would soon be well again. Instead, he spoke from the depths of his soul, "Jacob, I already have, with all of my heart."

Receiving the forgiveness he so desperately desired, Jacob Marley squeezed his friend's hand and fell back into a deep sleep. Robert left his home silently, knowing he would never see Mr. Marley again. As he left Marley's home and walked toward his own, he heard the carolers singing at the doors about town, which reminded him that tomorrow would be Christmas Eve. He wiped the tears from his eyes, thinking of the friend he was losing, but then smiled at the thought of Christmas Day with his good wife and children.

During the day of Christmas Eve, Mrs. Dilber, the charwoman who cleaned for Mr. Marley, meekly entered the business and spoke directly to Robert. "Pardon me, your kind sir. I have just come from Mr. Marley's and was asked to deliver a message to Mr. Scrooge."

Mrs. Dilber noticed Mr. Scrooge in his office behind his desk, as Robert replied in a quiet voice, "Yes, I will deliver your message."

"Thank you, your kind sir," she said, relieved she did not need to speak to Scrooge directly. "The message is that if Mr. Scrooge would like to take his leave of Mr. Marley, then he should come along smartly, while there's still someone to take leave of."

"Tsk, tsk," replied Robert, realizing the end was near for his employer. "I shall inform Mr. Scrooge at once."

Mrs. Dilber kept her place and listened to the conversation as best she could, after Robert scurried into Mr. Scrooge's office. "Pardon me, Mr. Scrooge?"

Scrooge looked up from his writing to see Robert standing before him, and a tattered old woman beyond him standing next to Robert's desk. "Yes? Well, what is it?"

"A message for you, sir, from the woman caring for Mr. Marley. She asks you to come at once to Mr. Marley's. I'm sorry to say he's dying, sir."

Scrooge acted no more concerned than if he had just been told that it might rain the following day. "Well? If he's dying, he's dying, what do you want me to do about it?"

Robert lowered his voice and spoke more directly, as if to make his own point. "Sir, this may be your last chance to speak with Mr. Marley."

More annoyed than concerned, Scrooge responded in a condescending manner. "We all have to die sometime, Cratchit." Then looking at the clock on the wall, Scrooge capitulated. "It is now half past three. The office is open until five. I will go then."

Scrooge returned to his writing without emotion. Robert returned to the outer room to tell Mrs. Dilber what she already knew from the pieces of the conversation she'd overheard. "Mr. Scrooge will come at five o'clock."

"I'll try to get him to hold on that long, I'm sure," replied Mrs. Dilber, showing her obvious displeasure by the tone of her voice at Scrooge's callousness. She showed herself to the door, and prepared to make her way back through the frigid afternoon breeze. Stopping before exiting, she turned to Robert, "Oh, and Merry Christmas, if it ain't in keeping with the situation."

To which Robert replied with a smile, "Yes, thank you, my dear, and Merry Christmas to you, as well." Robert returned to his work, disturbed by the news of Marley's dire condition. *How sad,* Robert thought, *that Mr. Marley might die on Christmas Eve.*

Within the same hour, the door to the business once again opened to a finely dressed gentleman. Robert approached the man from behind, helping him off with his coat and hat before he turned to face Robert, who instantly greeted the young man with a smile. "Fred Holloway!"

Fred pulled his finger to his lips in an effort to hush Robert. He walked past Robert with a wink and pat on the back to let himself into Scrooge's office without the customary introduction from his clerk.

Scrooge saw the stranger walk into his office, but didn't recognize the man. "Eh? Who's that?"

"'Tis I, Uncle, your nephew, Fred."

"Nephew?" Scrooge responded in a raspy, paranoid voice. "What do you want with me?"

"I want nothing of you, or from you, Uncle—merely to invite you to dine with me and my wife tomorrow for Christmas dinner."

"Bah!" Scrooge replied with his worst mannerism.

"Oh, please, Uncle. I hardly know you and my wife has never met you. We would both *very* much like to right that wrong by inviting you to dinner at our home."

"Thank you, no," replied Scrooge. "I am a busy man these days. My partner is not well and I carry the burden of the business on my own."

"But surely," Fred pressed, "you can take time on Christmas Day for a fine meal with family."

"Bah, family!" Scrooge lashed back, annoyed that this conversation was not yet over. "And Christmas—humbug!"

"Oh, surely you don't mean-..."

"Good day, sir!" Scrooge interrupted.

This exchange was no surprise to Fred, because the few chance meetings the two men had shared in the past ended similarly. Doing what he could to hold to his own positive attitude, Fred replied, "Well, the invitation stands, dear Uncle. I shall try again some other day."

"Bah!"

As he returned to the outer room where Robert stood, still holding Fred's coat and hat, he initiated a conversation. "Good to see you again, Robert."

"So good to see you, as well, Mr. Holloway."

Pulling on his coat with Robert's help, he corrected him, "Fred. Please Robert, Fred."

"Yes, sir, Fred. Please forgive Mr. Scrooge, sir. He really is having a bad time of it. You see, his partner is dying, not expected to even make it through the night."

"I'm heartily sorry to hear such news, especially on Christmas Eve," Fred replied. Peering into Scrooge's office, he challenged Robert's defense. "Yet I dare say, I think it would take more than the death of a business partner to rattle the bones of that old buzzard. In the years you have served my uncle, have you ever known him to show compassion or remorse, Robert?"

Unwilling to express any contempt toward Mr. Scrooge in the very office where he was employed, Robert quickly changed the subject, "How is your lovely wife, Mr.-... I mean, Fred?"

Fred smiled as he answered, "She is fine. I will be sure to tell her you asked in kind. And your wife and family, all ready for Christmas, I pray?"

"Oh yes, sir, all fine, as well, and anxious for a Christmas goose."

The two men exchanged well wishes for a festive Christmas. Before parting, Robert reminded Fred once more. "Please, Fred, don't give up on your uncle. Someday, he is bound to accept your invitation."

Fred smiled and shook Robert's hand while promising, "I will, sir. I will try and try again, until he accepts my invitation, or chokes to death on his own words of contempt."

"A moment of your time, Mr. Scrooge?" Robert asked, as Scrooge dressed to leave at the end of the day.

"Yes, what is it, Cratchit?" Scrooge inquired, disgusted that his evening routine was now at risk to resolve some issue for his clerk.

"Sir, I was wondering if the office might be closed tomorrow, being Christmas Day and all, sir."

Scrooge took his top hat from Robert, who was holding it for him as he dressed his scarf. He looked his clerk over from head to toe and back to head with a sneer on his upper lip, and finally replied with disdain, "And why, Mr. Cratchit, should I pay you a day's wages for no work? Answer me that, Mr. Cratchit!"

"'Tis only once a year, sir. It's more for the children and family than for myself, sir. They look so forward to this day all year."

"So, because you have a family, I am bound to pay for your merriment? Is that your excuse for picking my pocket, Mr. Cratchit?"

Robert stood silently as he tentatively buttoned the front of Scrooge's coat, hoping his employer would relent this day, as he had in years past.

"Be here all the earlier the next day, Cratchit!" Scrooge demanded, knowing he would make up for the lost time in the coming weeks by working his clerk harder and later.

"Thank you sir, thank you, indeed! That is most generous of you," replied Robert.

"Yes, I know it is. You don't have to tell me," came Scrooge's coarse response.

Adjusting Scrooge's collar, Robert thought of the man he had known for all these years, but had really only come to know in the last few weeks, "I pray you will find Mr. Marley well, sir."

Scrooge looked Robert in the eyes without an inkling of compassion. "I seriously doubt that a dying man can ever be *well*, Mr. Cratchit." Scrooge left the business, disturbed that his usual dinner time would be disrupted, but satisfied in the knowledge he would soon be the sole proprietor of Scrooge and Marley.

Chapter 16

Mr. Marley had been dead for four months, and spring was in the air. This meant the walk home from work was not only warmer for Robert, but daylight kept the night at bay until he entered his home. He walked slowly by the market, noticing the vegetable stands were not yet touting spring produce. "Robert," came a whispered voice. Turning in his tracks to see who called his name, he saw other Londoners, but no one who might have addressed him.

Must be someone else nearby named Robert, was his only thought, as he dismissed the distraction.

It was a day and a half later, when Robert was approaching Scrooge's office to begin another work day as he walked steadily through the morning fog that concealed London from sight, when he heard the same voice—yet this time he could not pass off the sound as a voice in the crowd, as there was no crowd about. "Robert, 'tis I, Jacob Marley." Fainter still, he heard many whispering voices. He could understand only a few words from the voices talking over one another. *"Tell him —ask him —help, please help —he won't do it —he must."* Slowly, the voices faded away.

Robert stopped dead in his tracks and turned completely around, seeing no one close enough to him to have made the sounds. A shiver ran from his head to his toes, as he felt a sudden chill and the hairs on his arms stand on end. "Mr. Marley?" he spoke, fearful someone might actually respond in kind.

Silence.

Robert quickened his pace to the office, checking over his shoulders constantly, but for what he was not certain. He opened the office, nervous to be alone, nearly wishing for Mr. Scrooge's company, no matter how distasteful it typically was. Half of the day was behind him before he could convince himself the voices he had heard were surely his imagination.

Scrooge left work early, as he customarily did every Wednesday, to scout business opportunities at the London Exchange. Once again, Robert found himself alone, as he diligently transcribed some letters Scrooge had left for him. Eerily, the hairs on the back of his neck stood, electrified by the sense of dread, followed by a cold chill that caused him to shiver.

The quill in his hand quivered when he first heard the whispering voices, and then heard the now familiar voice call his name for a third time, "Robert."

Not knowing how to hide from a voice that may just as well have come from inside his own head, as he could place no direction on the source of the sound, he mustered the strength to respond, "Who calls me?"

Several moments of silence followed, as he looked about the office from his desk when he felt another cold chill that seemed to pass through him, rather than around him. With a fleeting glance, he saw a shadowy movement in the mirror that hung near the front entry, but turning quickly to the mirror to face it head on revealed no unexpected reflection. Again, with no obvious source, he heard, "'Tis I, Jacob Marley." This time, the voice replied with a ghostly tone that sounded as though it was spoken from deep within a well.

Robert's chair tipped over, as he stood and backed himself into the corner of the room, where at least no one could approach him from behind. He exclaimed, "The dickens you are!" A moment passed, as Robert contemplated the voice's claim to an identity.

Then he challenged, "Jacob!" gulping air, as his mouth was suddenly dry. "That is, Mr. Marley is dead. He died four months ago."

Wide-eyed, he scanned the room, straining to see who might play such a cruel prank.

A full minute, which seemed like thirty, passed before he heard, "Nevertheless, 'tis I, Jacob Marley." The voice which began with a haunting tone seemed to sound clearer, and indeed more similar to Marley's, as the whispering voices faded away.

"I hear you, but I dare say I do not see you."

Responding quicker now, the voice replied, "You cannot see me."

"Why haunt me?"

Jacob's spirit wished to comfort Robert. "Nay, I do not haunt you, Robert. To the contrary, I beg your pardon and seek your help."

Robert was suddenly aware of his heart pounding, not only in his chest, but in both ears, as well. Terrified by the prospect of communicating with a spirit, he wanted to run, to escape the attention of the spirit that somehow broke through to his world from the realm of the afterlife.

"Do not flee, I *implore* you," came the voice of Marley.

Robert realized he could no more hide his thoughts than his body, from the spirit in the room. "You seek my help, Jacob? What is it you want from me?" Robert's pulse slowed, as he suddenly felt no sense of threat or impending doom from the spirit.

"I know not how long I will be able to speak with you Robert, so I must speak while I can."

"Yes?" responded Robert, as though he was carrying on a conversation with a visitor to the office. "But how do I know you are indeed the spirit of the man I once knew?"

"Your left hand was maimed by my greed and temperament."

"True, spirit," he replied, still not convinced the spirit was who he claimed. "Many know how my hand was crippled."

To prove his identity, Marley's ghost told Robert something only he would know. "You forgave me, Robert. I asked for your forgiveness, and you granted it."

"Saints be praised," Robert exclaimed, finally convinced his former employer and recent friend was indeed with him. "Tell me, what is it you want of me?"

"I know, now, what I was too blind to see in life, Robert Cratchit. I know, now, all of the kind deeds you have done for friend and stranger alike. I can see the ripples of your kindness and generosity, and it is a beautiful sight to behold. Had I been more like you in life, I would not be here begging your pardon in death. I am caught between your world and the next, and I am not alone. There are countless spirits who lament with me. All, like me, seek to right the wrongs that have trapped us in this lonely abyss."

Robert listened intently as Jacob continued, "We try, to no avail, to help the poor and destitute, but alas, we haven't the power. Many times I have called out to you on the street, in your home, and even in your dreams —but you hear me not."

Once again, Robert shivered at the thought of a spirit following him through the day, without his sense or knowledge.

"It is within every one of us the power to aid his fellow man exists. It is for each of us to use this power, if not in life, then we are condemned to do so in death. I wasted my life in this very business, turning my back on the needy and destroying lives with my own greed. I cannot move on to the next plane of existence, Robert, until I have fulfilled my lot."

"But how, Jacob? How can you right a wrong-... from where you are now?"

"With your help, Robert, I will, from time to time, guide you to a soul in need. When you give comfort or care to someone on my behalf, you bless me, as well. Please, do not fear me, my friend. I mean you no harm."

"I will help where I can, Jacob. I promise you, I will.

Silence.

"Jacob Marley?"

Silence.

How true, he thought, *my father's lessons of good versus evil must have been. Marley's life was filled with so much pain toward others that now he is tormented in death.*

Robert felt sad for the now deceased Marley. He finished his work for Scrooge and closed the office, remembering how frightened he had been when he'd opened the office that very morning.

As he began on his journey home, Robert decided to speak to no one, not even his dear wife, about his conversation with Jacob's spirit. *If word spreads about my talking with the dead, only bad will follow,* he thought. *Of this I'm certain. Being known as one who speaks to the dead would draw condemnation from many, while I'd also be hounded by others to contact their deceased relatives. No, this must remain secret, for my own welfare, as well as my family's.*

Walking through the street market, he suddenly felt as though he walked through the web of a spider, or more to the point, a web passed through him, when he heard, "Robert, pull a button from your coat and give it to the woman carrying a basket of bread."

"Sir?" he replied, looking all around himself for a sign of Marley.

Robert stopped beside a clothing shop and pulled the bottom button from his coat, wondering if he was actually losing his mind. Moments later, a woman with graying hair and a hunched shoulder passed directly in front of him, carrying a basket with two loaves of bread. "Here, madam," Robert said, reaching his hand out with the button between his fingers. "This is for you."

The woman stopped and took the button from Robert, who turned and walked away, so that he would not have to answer the inevitable questions about why he gave a stranger a button. Somehow, the old woman caught him before he could put distance between them, grabbed his arm, and pulled him around to face her. "Excuse me, sir." She looked Robert in the eyes and held the button out in her hand, "Why did you give me this?"

There really was no answer to the question that could possibly be believable, so he answered her question with one of his own. "Do you not know, my dear?"

Then she asked a question that was equally puzzling. "Did you know my husband?"

"I dare say no, at least not that I am aware."

The woman just stood there, staring into his eyes, as Robert watched hers fill with tears. "My husband died two weeks ago. Just before he died, I told him I could not live without him. He told me, before he passed, that if I find a button on the street, it would be his way of telling me he is happy, and that I will be, too. You see, his nickname for me over the last forty years was 'Button.' So I have been walking this neighborhood for the last two weeks, looking everywhere to find a button."

Robert took her hand, closed her fingers around the button and said, "Then he is happy now, and he wants you to be happy, too."

Robert left the woman with her button and walked home with a feeling of contentment. Content, not only for bringing some peace and happiness to an old, sweet lady, but content, as well, to know for certain that Jacob Marley was more real now than he ever had been during his life. Unsure if Mr. Marley would hear him or not, Robert still spoke to him aloud, "Nice one, Jacob."

Chapter 17

Staring through the front window of a local bakery, Stuart Simms didn't notice the mare as she walked up on him from behind. It wasn't until she nudged his back with her nose that he even knew he had company. Turning to see who had pushed him, he smiled at the insistence of the stranger and asked, "Hey girl, do I know you?"

The mare snorted and pressed her nose against his arm for attention. Stuart rubbed her mane down to her nose, and then pulled up the loose reins dangling from her bridle. "Looks to me like you came untied, girl. You better stay put until your master finds you."

Stuart continued into the market square, mentally rehearsing the list of goods to buy, as detailed by his wife, Anna. When he finally stood before the vegetable vendor, he said, "I need four carrots and six turnips," unfamiliar with the standard practice of picking the produce for purchase oneself and handing it to the vendor for bagging.

"I don't believe I've seen you here before," the vendor politely observed, as he picked the vegetables from his display box for Stuart to see.

"No, sir, normally my wife takes care of these matters. But she just delivered our second child, so I am out and about on the errands she gave me."

"Well, congratulations on the new baby! I can tell this must be your first attempt at shopping, else you would have known to tie your mare away from the market."

Stuart looked inquisitively at the vendor who motioned with his head to a horse standing just behind him. Stuart turned to see the same mare had followed him into the market. He chuckled, "I thought I told you to stay put!"

Looking back at the vendor, he shook his head and said, "Better make that *five* carrots. I'm dreadfully sorry, sir. I didn't know she would follow me here. I'll take her back and tie her securely."

Stuart thanked the vendor and took his vegetables, along with the reins of the lost horse, and walked her back to where they'd first met. Feeding her the carrot as they walked, he explained to the docile horse, "Now see here, your master will come along soon enough. So until then, I will tie you where he can find you."

From the corner of the next block, Stuart heard the anxious voice of a man yelling, "There she is! That man stole her! Arrest that man!"

Stuart stopped in his tracks, realizing the man running in his direction must surely be the horse's owner. In front of the man ran a constable. As the two rapidly approached, Stuart tried to ease the situation by holding the reins out for the owner, "She must be yours. She was loose and-..."

Before he could finish his sentence, the constable rammed his stick into Stuart's stomach and smacked him on his back after he'd doubled over.

The horse's owner demanded, "I want this horse thief arrested and hung!"

"I can arrest him," the constable responded, "but it will be up to the courts to hang him."

With the wind knocked out of him, dazed, and on his knees with his nose nearly touching the cobblestone street, Stuart tried to explain, "I didn't steal your horse; I swear it!"

"Quiet, you! I don't tolerate horse thieves in my jurisdiction."

"But I can prove it, sir!" Stuart proclaimed in his own defense, lifting his head, but remaining on his knees. "Just go ask that vegetable man! He will tell you! She was wandering loose and came to me while I was talking to him."

"Don't listen to that horse thief!" the horse's master insisted. "He'll say anything, now that he's caught!"

"Sir," the constable said, attempting to maintain control of the situation, "I will decide how to handle this crime. You wait here with your horse."

Grabbing the back of Stuart's shirt, the constable yanked up hard to pull him to his feet, "Come on you, we'll go talk to your vegetable man! But if you make one wrong move, I swear by God, I will split your skull open!"

The constable kept a firm clasp on the back of Stuart's shirt, as they walked briskly to the vegetable stand. "Good day, sir," the constable said, addressing the vendor, who had watched the entire arrest scene. "Do you recognize this man?"

"I do, yes sir, I do indeed."

"He claims you can vouch for him and that he never had possession of the horse over there. Are you willing to swear to the magistrate that he did not steal the horse?"

"No sir, I cannot swear to that. No sir, not at all," the vendor answered nervously, fearing himself being drawn into a serious crime. "He talked to the horse like she was his, even bought a carrot to feed her."

"I've heard *enough*," the constable replied, now convinced he had a horse thief by the collar. "I'm sorry to trouble you, sir."

"But that's not what-..." Stuart got four words out before being beat viciously again. The vendor cringed, as he watched the constable slam his stick across Stuart's chest.

"I thought I told you to be quiet!"

Standing before a bench of five judges in powdered wigs and black robes, Stuart wore wrist and ankle shackles, while listening to the verdict that would change his life forever, "Mr. Simms, in the face of overwhelming evidence and eyewitness testimony, this court has found you guilty of theft of property. As officers of the court representing his majesty the King of England, we will now pass your sentence. Theft of a horse is a capital offense, punishable by death. However, as no evidence has been brought before this court that proves you took the animal, we can only convict you for possession of stolen property. You are hereby sentenced to five years imprisonment."

The slamming of the gavel on the bench felt like a stake piercing his heart. Stuart turned to take one last look at Anna, who sat in the courtroom, crying as silently as she could. Stuart also got his last glance at his children, since she was holding their six-week-old baby, while their three-year-old son sat by her side.

Standing beneath the "Scrooge & Marley" office sign that moved slightly with the breeze, Robert saw it—now freshly painted—as it must have looked when it was first hung. From the street, he could distinguish the silhouette of a man in the front window, but a moment later, the figure moved to the front door and exited onto the street in front of the office. "Who tied this horse here in front of my door?!" the man yelled.

Looking first one way, then the other, a young Jacob Marley waited for the owner of the horse to appear. "Very well, then!" he yelled as a final warning, before untying the horse's reins from the railing in front of his business and slapping the mare on the rump to send her away.

Robert suddenly woke, with a feeling of complete doom bringing him back to consciousness. His bedroom was still dark, but he knew morning was approaching, as he could hear the lamp lighters make their way down the street, snuffing out the street lamps, one after the other.

So real, he thought to himself. *I don't remember ever having such a vivid dream!* Lying in bed, he reflected on the many details of his lengthy dream, details that did not easily fade from memory. At morning's light, he wrote the names Stuart and Anna Simms on a piece of paper. *If this dream was a foretelling of events to come,* he thought, *then I may find an opportunity to warn them, if our paths cross. If, on the other hand, this dream was of events already passed, then may God save that innocent man and his family.*

Walking to work, Robert found himself studying the faces of strangers, looking for either Mr. or Mrs. Simms, at least as he knew them in his dream. *A dream of people I do not know,* he surmised, *is surely a foreshadowing of things to come.*

Chapter 18

Robert slowly grew accustomed to the feeling of being watched. He was not certain whether Jacob Marley's spirit was "attached" to him, following him everywhere he went, or if he wandered the spirit world, contacting Robert as needed. For peace of mind, if such peace was possible for a man who was regularly contacted by a spirit of the dead, Robert assumed that Jacob was always by his side. On occasion, he would even talk to Jacob, when he knew he could talk without being heard by any *living* soul. Jacob would rarely answer Robert, at least not in any conversation Robert initiated. Still, it gave him a sense of peace to think of Jacob Marley as a sort of "personal spirit guide," as it were.

Sometimes months would go by without contact—so much so that Robert would wonder if Jacob had moved on, or at least lost the ability to communicate with him. Then, usually at the most unexpected moment, he would hear his friend and former employer go on at him about this or that, making Robert consider him more of a companion than a lost soul.

"Robert, go to the bakery and wait by the back door for the baker to give you some bread."

As with so many encounters with Jacob over the course of time since his passing, Robert learned it was futile to question him. Early on, when he did, he was rarely granted a response. So, on his way home from work, Robert found himself standing in the alley by the back door of the bakery for only a few minutes, when suddenly the door opened. Surprised by Robert's presence, the baker addressed his regular customer. "Mr. Cratchit? What brings you to my back door? Please, come around front where I can serve you. I was just throwing some bread out for the dogs."

"Thank you, Mr. Danbury," Robert responded. "But if you're throwing the bread out, might I have it, instead?"

The baker looked at the pieces of bread in his hand, and then offered it to him. "You certainly may, sir, but this bread broke while I was taking it from the fire. Wouldn't you like a finer looking loaf than these scraps?"

"You bake the best bread in London. I know this to be true," Robert replied, "but just this once, I have need of your scraps."

Mr. Danbury, who had helped Robert on many occasions with gifts for the homeless, handed the bread to Robert. "Then please, take this for your generous service, Mr. Cratchit."

The baker filled Robert's pockets and coat with scraps, and in return, received Robert's heartfelt gratitude. Robert walked from the alley to the street, where he immediately heard Jacob's voice say, "Trade the bread for five flowers."

On the next block, standing on the corner, Robert saw a raggedy little blond-haired girl selling flowers from her basket. A thick fog, visible to no other, seeped through the mortar that held the bricks to the wall behind her. Through the falling mist, a shadowy figure of a man formed, earnestly pointing to the child.

"Hello, my dear. I have no money, but I wonder if you would be interested in trading some flowers for fresh bread?" He pulled some bread from his pockets with both hands.

The girl's face lit up, as she exclaimed, "Yes, indeed, sir!"

Robert extracted the equivalent of two or three small, but hearty loaves from his pockets, and all he had been able to carry within his coat. With a smile, he held the bread in front of himself for the girl to see.

"Sir, you may have *all* of my flowers in return!"

Robert chuckled at the thought, but responded, "Thank you kindly, my dear. Your flowers are most beautiful, but I would like for you to pick out just five of your prettiest flowers for me."

The child intently studied her basket of flowers and pulled out five daisies, wrapped them in paper with care, and held them out to Robert. "Oh, that is lovely, sweetheart. I am most grateful." In a few seconds, he'd filled the girl's basket with bread and gently took the five flowers from her hand.

"And thank you in return, kind sir." Staring at the edible treasure she now possessed, she hefted up her basket of bread and the remaining flowers, and then hurried across the street.

Robert continued to walk in the direction of home, reflecting on Jacob's most recent request. The closer he got to home, the more concerned he was that he had somehow missed *all* of Jacob's instructions. He stood outside the door to his home, paused and looked around. No one approached him. No words from his spirit companion. "Jacob?"

Silence.

Not knowing what else to do, he entered his home, flowers in hand, and soon stood face-to-face with Emily, who he greeted with a kiss.

"Here, what's this?" Emily inquired, noticing he had something wrapped in his hands.

Still confused by his loss of contact with Jacob, Robert handed the cone-shaped package to his wife without saying a word.

Emily unrolled the paper to reveal the five hand selected daisies, and then opened her mouth wide. She threw her arms around her husband, who had barely time to hang his coat on a hook after taking it off. Emily kissed him once on each cheek and then passionately on his lips. She held him close to her, with her arms tightly around him. "After you left this morning, I thought you had forgotten our anniversary for sure!"

Robert looked at the flowers lying on the table, returned his wife's hug, and closed his eyes, thinking, *Our anniversary! Of course! Thank you, Jacob. Thank you!*

Emily proceeded to tell Robert, with excitement, about her day. "Martha asked me this morning if you had remembered the day, but I passed her off by telling her our five children are the blessings that remind me of our anniversary every day of our lives, not just this blessed date. And then I thought to myself that, if you felt as I do, maybe you *might* do something to celebrate our family. It is as if you could read my mind, dear Robert. Five daisies, my *favorite* flower—one for each of our five blessings."

"Yes, indeed." Robert smiled at both his wife and his good fortune to have been rescued by his spirit companion, who had apparently been promoted to 'guardian angel' this day. "Happy anniversary, my love," he said, prefacing the next kiss.

It was apparent to Robert the flowers brought great joy to his wife. What he could not see, and could not know, were the ripples unfolding before Marley, as he followed the flower girl with her basket of bread and flowers.

Inside the shelter for homeless women, the girl found her mother on the floor, leaning against the wall with their few meager possessions next to her, holding her listless eight-month-old son in her arms. "Mother, look what I have!" the girl said, happily showing her the bread.

"God bless you, Mary," her mother responded, taking a small piece of bread from the basket. As her son was severely dehydrated from fever, he could no longer suckle his mother. "Hand me a bowl, my love."

In the bowl retrieved for her, Mary's mother excreted milk from her breast, and then touched the piece of bread to the white liquid. "Let's see if he'll take it like this," she said, partly to Mary and partly to herself. As she touched the soggy bread to her infant's mouth, sliding it back and forth across his cracked lips, both she and her daughter gasped, seeing his lips part and close to receive a single drop of nourishment.

Mary moved closer, so that her face was nearly touching her brother's, as she watched him take more and more of his mother's milk from the softened bread. Leaching into the milk were the nutrients from the grains that had been milled into the finest bread in London.

As Jacob's spirit hovered above the desperate family, he felt the love from all three for the kindness they'd received from a stranger. A veil that had always been before him suddenly parted, allowing him to witness the future years, where brother and sister spent time playing together, and even beyond, where the boy would one day have a family of his own, and onward, into a vision of the countless generations to follow.

Chapter 19

Nigel walked with his wife, Cassandra, and their daughter, Krystin, through the alley behind the restaurants, looking for discarded food scraps that the rats had not yet discovered. "Two pieces of bread," Nigel said, staring at the partially eaten scraps in his hands. "Not much for three people."

"We'll be alright, Nigel," Cassandra said, trying to comfort her husband. "We just have to give it time. You'll find work again, my dear, I know you will."

"If I don't find work soon, we'll starve! You really picked a winner when you chose me, Love."

"Please don't talk that way." Looking at their six-year-old daughter standing next to her, she added, "You upset Krystin and you upset me when you say such things! Let's go home, now. I still have a couple of potatoes I can boil."

Slowly they progressed through the streets toward their home, picking up anything that could be eaten or sold along the way. "What is it, Mummy?" Krystin asked, as her parents stopped outside their home.

Both Nigel and Cassandra stood at the stoop to their front door without entering. "What does it say?" Krystin asked again of her parents, who stared at the eviction notice nailed to their door.

Krystin broke through the silence of shock, "I'm hungry. Can't we go inside?"

Her father and mother turned to look at one another. "Not today, my love," Nigel responded. "Not today."

Near them, in the road where they stood, were the few meager possessions that even their neighbors didn't want after picking through their belongings. The three turned and walked away slowly, knowing they could never return. In a nearby tunnel, where homeless were known to sleep, the family huddled and shared the morsels of bread with each other. Afraid to sleep for fear of harm from another desperate soul, Nigel stayed awake most of the night, while Cassandra and Kristen slept in each other's arms.

"Here . . . for the child." A stranger's voice woke Nigel and Cassandra, who looked up to see an old woman holding a tin cup for them. Motioning again with the cup, she explained, "I ain't seen you here before. I found some chicken bones yesterday and boiled them into a broth. Go ahead, take it. I ain't going to hurt you."

Cassandra took the cup, "Bless you, dear lady."

"Yes, thank you, my dear," Nigel said. "She hasn't eaten for two days now."

As the kind stranger retreated to her cooking fire across the tunnel, Nigel spoke to Cassandra with conviction. "I want you and Krystin to go to your parent's home tomorrow. They'll take the two of you in."

"No, Nigel. We stay together. You come with us and I will talk to my father about letting all three of us stay there."

"Your father will have nothing to do with me, but I'm sure he'll take you and Krystin. Besides, it will be easier for me to find work, if I know you both are well cared for."

Across the street from her parent's home, Cassandra embraced her husband as they prepared to separate. "It won't be long, Casey," Nigel said with his most feeble attempt to reassure his wife. "Once I find steady work, I will come for you and Krystin. We will be a family again, you'll see."

With more tears than words on her lips, Cassandra held her daughter's hand to cross the quiet, upscale street to the polished home of her parents. Nigel watched from the shadows as the silver-haired, robust gentleman opened the door and spoke rather coldly to his daughter. Moments later, Cassandra and Kristin walked past the man, into the stately manor, who offered no expression of emotion to the daughter he had not seen in nearly seven years, or the granddaughter he had never met. Instead, he only looked in both directions of the street to insure his daughter and granddaughter were indeed alone.

For weeks, Nigel waited at noon beneath the bell tower at the church near the home of Cassandra's parents, where she brought him food scraps, which she'd salvaged from her parent's table. Every day, the couple would talk, while he ate the morsels of food she'd brought. Every day, Nigel felt he was closer to finding work. Every day, the couple would part with an embrace and a promise of better days ahead.

As the weeks became months, Cassandra began missing their noon rendezvous, blaming her parents for interfering with her daily meeting. One day, unbeknownst to her husband, it was her last visit with him.

After two weeks of waiting for the wife who never showed, Nigel went to Cassandra's home and witnessed the gut-wrenching scene he feared. From the shadows across the street, he watched as Cassandra and Krystin climbed into the carriage of a well-dressed suitor who kissed his wife, as she took her place next to him.

The following day, just after the hour of noon, a local constable was called to remove the body of a homeless man who was hanging by the neck beneath the bell tower next to the church.

A shadowy man wandered through a small flat, tossing one item after another through the open door. Everything that wasn't nailed down went flying out, until both rooms were completely empty. Then, standing at the front entrance after closing the door behind him, he hammered a nail on the wooden door. As the man turned to walk away, his face struck a chord of familiarity. It was Jacob Marley, as a young, ambitious business man. Impervious to the pain or suffering of others, the man who hammered the nail that held the eviction notice was a man of singular purpose: maximize profits, no matter the cost.

Robert opened his eyes following this, another nightmare. The emotionally charged dream left him exhausted and with an overwhelming feeling of depression. He rubbed his throat and tried to clear the taste of blood from his mouth.

Just as with previous nightmares, this dream was hauntingly realistic. *How can I possibly interpret the message*, Robert wondered. *Is the demise of Nigel something I caused, or will cause?*

Wrapping an arm around his wife, Robert tried to overcome the feelings of despair by reassuring himself he was blessed with the undying love of a good woman.

In the stillness of night, Emily woke to her husband tossing and turning. "Robert," she whispered in the darkness. "Are you alright? Are you having trouble sleeping?"

"Yes, I'm sorry I woke you, Emily," Robert whispered in response. "I just had a bad dream. I'm fine now."

In the morning light, he pulled the piece of paper from his shirt pocket that had the names of Stuart and Anna Simms, and added three more names; Nigel, Cassandra, and Krystin.

Chapter 20

Through the years, Robert noticed the Christmas season was when Jacob Marley was most active. For some, Christmas was a time for celebration with family and friends. For others, Christmas was a time for reflection. Still others suffered for lack of the most basic necessities and companionship. It was for those who suffered that Jacob Marley took pity and embraced in death, although he had ignored them during his life.

One wintery day, as the door to the business opened, Robert instinctively rose from his seat to welcome the visitor. Fred Holloway gestured to Robert to remain silent, as he pulled his hat and scarf off to hang on the rack, even though it was nearly as cold inside as out. Robert greeted Mr. Scrooge's nephew with a silent smile and nod, as he lifted Fred's overcoat from his shoulders to hang by his hat and scarf.

Fred winked at Robert and gathered himself for his yearly joust with his uncle. Breaking the relative silence of the office, Fred startled Scrooge with a loud, "Merry Christmas, Uncle!"

Scrooge shifted his quill as he flinched, drawing a heavy black line on his writing pad. Angry at being startled and angrier still that he must start over with his letter, Scrooge lashed back, "Nephew!"

"Uncle," Fred continued, undeterred by the old man's bitterness, "I have come to remind you that Christmas Eve is upon us, and to invite you to dine with my wife and me tomorrow for Christmas dinner."

Robert treasured the show Fred gave him every year and listened to his invitation intently, as Fred countered every bitter response of Scrooge's with a pleasant gesture of his own. On this day, though, Robert's attention was diverted with the voice only he could hear, "Swap Fred's scarf for your own."

Robert acted without hesitation, all the while listening to the banter between Scrooge and his jovial nephew. "But why, Uncle? Every year I come here with good will in my heart and ask you only to share a Christmas meal and some of your time with us."

"I did not ask you to come here this Christmas Eve, or any other for that matter," countered Scrooge. "You have what is yours and I have what is mine. Leave well enough alone, Nephew."

"I will leave you as you wish, dear Uncle, but I can promise you I will never stop trying, until you accept my invitation. If not this year, then maybe the next."

"Good day, sir!" snapped Scrooge.

"Merry Christmas, Uncle."

"Bah!"

"And a Happy New Year, sir!"

"Humbug!"

Fred retreated to the outer office where Robert waited to help him don his coat, hat, and scarf. Scrooge's nephew did not notice he now wore a black scarf, having entered just moments earlier with a red one. Always the gentleman, he was easily distracted, busily reacquainting himself with Robert, asking about his wife and children.

After responding briefly, Robert inquired in turn. "And you, sir? Have you and Mrs. Holloway started a family of your own?"

The question made Fred slightly uneasy, and he hesitated for a moment. "No, not yet, sir. My wife has miscarried twice before, but seems unable to get pregnant now. It is a very sensitive matter with her, but I fear we must acknowledge children are not in our future."

"Oh, I'm very sorry, Fred," Robert exclaimed, embarrassed he had made Fred uncomfortable in their conversation. "I pray your good wife is well, physically and spiritually."

Fred smiled as he shook Robert's hand, "Yes, quite well, and I know she would love to see you again. Why don't you come for a visit sometime, Robert?"

"Thank you sir, I shall indeed. Merry Christmas, sir."

"And a Merry Christmas to you and all of the growing Cratchits!"

After his nephew had left, Scrooge sat working away, detesting the merriment and niceties on the lips of people he heard on the street outside his window. The music and laughter seemed phony. The nicer a stranger was to him, the more bitter he felt. Try as he might, he could not focus on his work with the sounds of carolers beyond the front door of his business. Convinced that children by his door would drive away prospective customers, he decided to drive the beggars away with his own form of Christmas spirit.

Flinging open the door, he yelled at a gathering of children, "Be gone!" The children scattered, as he heaved the small stone he used as a paper weight toward the center of the group. As the older children dodged the stone, it grazed the side of the head of the smallest child, a boy barely four years old.

The child fell to the ground and his sister knelt beside him. Robert did not witness the event, but heard the young girl call out for help. Running past Scrooge, who slammed the door behind him, Robert quickly reached the children and knelt beside the boy who was lying on his back in the snow. At nearly the same moment, another adult knelt beside Robert, angrily exclaiming, "That old buzzard could have killed this boy." Robert instantly recognized Fred Holloway's voice, but kept his attention focused on the child.

Blood trickled from the boy's forehead and swelling was pushing the cut open, but he was conscious and crying. "Thank goodness, he's awake," said Robert. "He'll be alright, I think."

Fred looked at the girl and asked, "Is this your brother?"

The girl, who could not have been more than seven years old, replied, "He is. Please leave him be. I'll take care of him."

Taken back by her abrupt response, Robert and Fred looked at each other. Robert asked, "Where are your parents, my dear?"

"Dead, they are." Robert and Fred both sat dumbfounded in the snow for a few heart-wrenching moments. Then, without a word, Fred drew the boy up and held him in his arms to comfort him.

"Who is caring for you then?" Robert eventually asked the boy's sister.

"I care for him, and he cares for me." The young girl stroked the face of the crying boy in Fred's arms.

Again, Fred and Robert looked at each other bewildered. Fred then asked, "Do you live in an orphanage?"

"No, we don't!" The girl reacted to his question as though she'd been asked if she'd been living in an ogre's cave. "They eat children in the orphanage, you know. They cook them and eat them."

Any other time, both Fred and Robert would have found her response comical, but in the dead of winter, this was a grave situation.

Fred lifted the boy and walked over to the steps in front of Scrooge's door, where he could sit with the two children away from pedestrians and horses. "Please, sit here while I see to it your brother is alright," Fred told the girl. "What are your names, dear?"

"I'm Allie and he's Adam."

Robert watched intently as Fred charmed this little girl who had lived on the streets for God alone knew how long. Before his very eyes, a bond between them was developing. Fred held little Adam in his lap and Allie sat close to him for warmth. Robert listened, as Fred inquired into the children's circumstances.

Gently, Fred asked, "Allie, would you like to come home with me? I would like for you to meet my wife, so she can tend to Adam's cut."

Allie looked up at Robert, who smiled and nodded with agreement. Turning her attention back to Fred, she asked, "Have you got food there?"

Fred laughed and said, "Yes, yes, I'm sure we can find plenty for you and Adam to eat."

The door swinging open startled both men and the two children. Allie clung tightly to Fred's coat, when she saw Scrooge step out. Ignoring his nephew and the children in his arms, he addressed Robert directly, while pointing the silver knob of his cane toward him. "Cratchit! Back to work!" Turning quickly, he slammed the door before Robert could respond.

Robert darted up the building's front stairs toward the door, past Fred and the children, then stopped and turned just before he opened the door. "Oh, Mr. Holloway, why did you come back? You left here over an hour ago."

"Oh my, I nearly forgot." Fred pulled his scarf off and handed it toward Robert, "Here, sir, I believe I left here with your scarf by mistake."

In time, Robert would learn what Jacob Marley already knew. Very shortly, Allie and Adam would be given the surname of Holloway.

Chapter 21

The pub was filled with loud, rutty sailors from lands near and far. The color of a man's skin or the shape of his eyes made no difference here—it was merely his strength and fortitude that defined him as a man of the sea. At the end of the bar, leaning on one elbow, was a large, bearded man with deep wrinkles in a face that had been beaten by sea spray for countless years. At his side sat a much younger, clean-shaven, muscular man. The two men swallowed a mouthful of dark ale and surveyed the smoky pub cautiously.

"Captain," began the first mate, "It's too risky, if you ask me. We don't have to take this shipment. There'll be others, you can be sure."

"Aye, Mate, and did you tell them no one sails for the Americas in the month of July?"

"I did, Captain, but the man was insistent. He offered to double the bounty, if we were in Norfolk in six weeks' time."

The captain took another drink and sat his mug back on the bar, swirling the ale in his mouth as he did. As the last of the foam bubbles disappeared from his lips, he declared, "Assemble the crew. We sail in two days on the high tide."

"Captain York?"

The captain turned to look through the pub's front window at the top of the mast of his ship, which was anchored in the bay. He took a deep breath through his nose and said, "We'll be alright, Banner. The seas are calm and the air is dry. We can catch the southern trades and slip in from the south. If need be, we'll stay anchored in Virginia until the threat of storms has passed."

Slowly the Schooner Constantine slipped through Bristol Harbor with jib sails fluttering in the breeze. Many of the deck hands not active in maneuvering the vessel stood on her starboard side looking for family, along the boardwalk, who came to bid the ship and souls aboard her *bon voyage*. "Is that your wife, Mr. Banner?" the young cabin boy asked while standing near the bow, next to the first mate, noticing the woman who returned his wave.

"Aye, lad. Twill be nary three months before I lay me eyes on her again."

"And the boy next to her, is that your son?" the inquisitive cabin boy pursued.

"Nay lad, we have no children of our own," Banner replied. "Maybe one day."

As the Constantine rode the wind into open waters, the cabin boy returned the wave from the young boy standing next to Mrs. Banner, imagining the family and friends the boy must surely have, yet he himself was so starkly denied.

The ship listed to port, when the wind suddenly shifted. Every man on deck stopped what he was doing to look at the sky. "Squall line to the southeast, Captain!" called out a distant voice from high up in the crow's nest.

"Ten degrees starboard!" Captain York called to the pilot.

"Ten degrees, aye, Captain!"

"You think we can outrun it, Captain?" asked the first mate.

"Outrun it or die trying, Mr. Banner."

The first mate, a seasoned sailor in his own right, with more than fifteen voyages alongside Captain York, sprang into action, "You men, take those crates below and secure them fast! I don't want to see anything on this ship's deck other than the men who serve her!"

As the wind picked up, the waves lifted the mighty vessel from the ocean's surface, as if handing her to the storm itself. Still, the first mate persevered, orchestrating all hands on deck. "Give me all three jibs! Make smart men! We're running with lower and coarse sails! Secure the topsail and staysail!"

As one of the sailors climbed down a rope from securing the topsail, a large wave broke over the bow and swept him overboard.

"Man overboard!" shouted the sailor from the crow's nest.

A driving rain whipped by the howling winds stung the exposed faces and hands of the crew who were now working hard simply to survive. The ship suddenly tossed starboard, followed by a loud crack of the fore mast, which fell quickly and hung dangling over the bow. Two men who were clinging to the topsail yard vanished before the vessel righted herself.

A few of the men, the unfortunate ones, clung to floating debris, as the remnants of the once mighty Constantine dispersed across the surface of the endless sea. The rest sank slowly into the depths of the dark water, the sea claiming one victim after another. As each man passed deeper, the faces of their wives, sons, and daughters appeared, drifting up through the ocean void.

One of the fallen sailors was a young cabin boy, serving on the ship because he had no other family. Beyond him came forward the face of the woman who would have been his wife, had he lived. Behind her were the faces of three children who would have been born, but now denied the opportunity for life. Behind *them* were the faces of eight grandchildren and the multitudes of generations that would have followed. Breaking through the silence of the watery cemetery came the conversation of two businessmen, "Gone? What do you mean *gone*?"

"Just that, Mr. Marley. The Constantine never arrived. There was a hurricane that hit the east coast of America and we believe she was caught by it. She never stood a chance, sir."

"Now, you see here," the voice of Jacob Marley began. "I told that captain to wait until *August* before making the crossing. If you wish to keep your home and your situation, you will have nothing more to say beyond that! Are we clear, sir?"

"Yes, Mr. Marley, perfectly clear."

"It's no matter," Marley added. "The shipment was insured, so nothing of importance was lost."

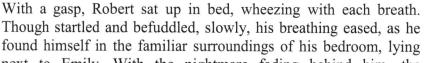

With a gasp, Robert sat up in bed, wheezing with each breath. Though startled and befuddled, slowly, his breathing eased, as he found himself in the familiar surroundings of his bedroom, lying next to Emily. With the nightmare fading behind him, the pounding in his chest receded. "How horrible," he whispered, remembering the details of every man's face that sank past him, while he hovered under the ocean's surface.

Holding Emily close, afraid to let go for fear of falling asleep, Robert's thoughts wandered in the darkness still left in the night. *What dreadful, yet shockingly realistic nightmares! What could they possibly mean? And will they ever stop or am I going mad?*

As he contemplated the various nights of terror-filled sleep, Robert felt the ghastly dreams coming together. *Jacob Marley released the mare that Stuart Simms was wrongly accused and convicted of stealing. Jacob Marley evicted Nigel, along with his wife and young daughter, from the home they could no longer afford. Jacob Marley ordered the shipment during the most life-threatening time of year, sending all the souls onboard the Constantine to a watery grave.*

Every vivid nightmare, he reasoned, *has followed on the heels of a day made all the better by Jacob Marley intervening for someone's sake.* Robert saw the common thread tying the nightmares quite clearly. With a whispering, raspy voice, he said, "Marley."

Seeing the young age of Marley in my dreams, Robert thought, *I must have been dreaming of events past. I wonder how real-to-life they actually were.*

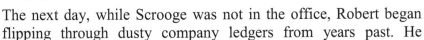

The next day, while Scrooge was not in the office, Robert began flipping through dusty company ledgers from years past. He searched every page of every year, going as far back as their records allowed.

At last, his diligence was rewarded. "Found you!" Robert shouted, upon coming to a name recorded in Jacob Marley's handwriting.

Nigel Clemens. Six weeks past due. Evicted.

In the following year's ledger came his next confirming clue, again in the handwriting of Jacob Marley.

July fifth, contracted Captain York to sail The HMS Constantine to Norfolk, Virginia. Outbound shipment: Forty barrels whiskey, porcelain, silver cutlery. Return shipment: Tobacco, cotton, Native American artifacts. Est. profit: £3500

So that's it, Robert concluded, closing the ledger and returning it to the shelf before Scrooge caught him studying company records. *I've been dreaming of Jacob Marley's past. But why am I being made to suffer, witnessing bad deeds Mr. Marley committed before I knew him?*

Speaking aloud to be heard by his ghostly companion, Robert inquired. "Why, Jacob-... why have I endured the visions of your past?"

"It is what it is," the ghostly voice replied. "With every good deed you perform on my behalf, a past sin is erased. You see in your dreams what I see, you suffer as I suffer. The pain I spread in life torments me in death. Your dreams are of my reality. Again, I beg your pardon."

"Please spirit," Robert pleaded, "haunt my dreams no more. I cannot bear the misery of that which you suffer."

Suddenly, as a child would commit a tantrum, Marley's cries surrounded Robert, coming from every corner of the room. The haunting screams and thunderous wailing terrified Robert who was barely accepting the presence of a ghostly spirit in his life. Beyond the wailing voice, chains rattled as if the anchor of a great sailing vessel suddenly crashed on the floor beneath him, followed by link after link of the tethered shackle. "Oh man of the Earth, have you no mercy?! Have you no pity?!" Marley cried out.

Robert was consumed with fright, fearing the wrath of an enraged ghost. Somehow, he found the strength of mind to challenge the angry spirit, "Jacob, you suffer the pain you brought to others in life! It is not right that I should be made to suffer the ripples of your decisions. You and you alone cast your stones upon the water."

The room filled with silence as Robert waited for a response that came moments later, in a calmer, more sorrowful tone, "Oh the pain Robert-... the pain." A sudden chill, as one would feel opening a door on a blustery night, consumed Robert as Marley's spirit passed through him. Marley's voice fell ever fainter as he kept repeating, "The pain-... the pain."

Chapter 22

Monday through Saturday, Robert Cratchit served Ebenezer Scrooge, but Sunday he served the Cratchit family. It was a Cratchit tradition he cherished, treasuring family time on Sunday, which always began with morning church services. Following church, cool or rainy days invited indoor games, songs, or storytelling. Warm days often led to picnics in the park or a stroll and some window shopping in the city.

It seemed like most weekends, street performers were on every corner in town, collecting coins for entertaining a crowd. Minstrels played instruments and sang songs. Jugglers and magicians did brief shows for children of all ages. Tiny Tim, in particular, enjoyed the family outings, mainly because he had the best place on the street to watch the entertainers—from atop his father's shoulders. At the end of each show, Robert would lower Tim to the ground and hand him a coin, which he'd proudly walk with (using his crutch) over to the hat that collected the performer's earnings.

Without question, the street performer who best captured the attention of every Cratchit was always the storyteller. It was not uncommon for one or more of the Cratchit children to entertain their siblings later that very day or during the week by trying their best to retell the story with all of the emotion and gestures they'd learned from the original.

"Gather around, my children, while I take you on a journey to a different time, a different place!" This was the most common way the performers would announce a new story was about to begin. Upon hearing these words, Martha would walk Tim to the front of the crowd, where the children would sit to be closest to the storyteller. Belinda and Richard sat with Tim, while Peter and Martha stood with their parents behind the children.

One particular Sunday, after hearing the announcement being called out, Robert and his family gathered around as close as they could to a thin woman in her fifties, dressed somewhat flamboyantly and with a wry smile in her crystal blue eyes. With a clear, loud voice that could be heard over the street sounds of pedestrians, horses and carts, she began.

"In a faraway place, where a king ruled over a land that was filled with all of the food imaginable, the people of the kingdom were happy—*except* for their fear of the dragon that lived in a cave by the shore." As her story unfolded, every person in the crowd was fixated on the woman's face and hands, as her facial expressions and well-crafted gestures told as much of the story as did her words.

The woman wove her story through the ears and hearts of everyone present, child and adult alike, taking on the personality of her characters as she paced or skipped back and forth before the crowd, while acting out each scene. For the next twenty minutes, every Cratchit was either the knight who fought the dragon, nearly losing his own life, or the king's beautiful daughter whose hand the knight would win, if he returned with the head of the dragon. The crowd erupted in applause when her story ended, as it had soulfully satisfied their wildest imaginations. As the throngs of people began dispersing after the show's conclusion, dozens of coins filled the bottom of her basket, which sat near her few belongings.

The woman watched Tiny Tim, as he stood with Richard's help, while Belinda held his crutch for him. She felt blessed that she was able to bring some fantasy into such a young life, who was obviously no stranger to pain. For her, the glow on Tiny Tim's face as she heard him say, "I thought for *sure* the knight was done for when the dragon found him in his cave," was a greater reward than the sum of coins lining her basket.

When Robert found his three youngest in the crowd, he gave each of the children a coin to drop into the storyteller's basket. As they did so, he approached the storyteller to tip his hat and thank her for such an entertaining adventure. With all of the Cratchit children gathered beside their parents, the woman thanked each of them individually for listening to her story. However, when she got to Robert, her smile went solemn, as she reached for his right hand and held it between her own two hands.

Looking directly into Robert's eyes for what became an uncomfortable moment for him, she twitched her head, as though recovering from a momentary lapse. "Someone is attached to you, but not of this world," she stated. "Good energy—nothing bad, not evil. Good energy." Then, as if returning from a trance, the woman once again smiled and shook Robert's hand, thanking him for listening to her story.

As he expected, they were only a few steps down the street before Emily asked, "What did she mean, Robert, about someone being attached to you?"

Robert knew exactly what the woman meant, though how she knew he had no clue. Still, he passed off his encounter with the storyteller to his wife. "I'm sure she noticed what a large and wonderful family we are, my dear."

"But she said it was not of this world. What did she mean by that?"

Not wishing to go into a deep discussion, he just dismissed the conversation as simply as he could. "She's a storyteller. She dramatizes everything. I'm sure it was merely her way of telling us how blessed we are to have each other."

A moment later, Robert was grateful for the smell of fresh baked bread coming from a bakery, as they passed by. Without effort, it turned everyone's attention, and the conversation, to speculate on how recently the bread had come out of the baker's oven.

On a different Sunday, in a different year, the Cratchits left church as they often did, walking through the cemetery to visit and care for Becky's grave.

"Father?" Tim asked, breaking the silence of the moment.

"Yes, my boy?"

"Is Grandmother in Heaven?"

"Most certainly, Tim. Why do you ask?"

"Just wondering, I suppose. The minister said today that all good people go to Heaven, and I know Grandmother was a good person."

Emily joined the conversation. "Truer words were never spoken."

Robert took his wife's fingers in his hands, as his way of thanking her for keeping his mother's memory alive. He then addressed the entire family. "Well, my children. What about a picnic in the park this fine spring day?"

Everyone approved of the idea, as each imagined how the day might unfold. Emily, in particular, enjoyed pulling together enough food to fill a basket, which they would carry to the park and eat under a tree. After making their way to the park with a basket packed with enough morsels to satisfy every Cratchit's belly, Emily spread out an old quilt, which typically hung over the rocking chair next to the fireplace, before sitting with her husband and the food basket between them.

Some of the children played games with each other, although Peter chose to join with some boys his own age in a game of keep-away. Tim stood a stone's throw away from his parents, balanced by his crutch, as he rooted for his oldest brother. Richard and Belinda climbed a tree and played "make believe," while Martha sat with her parents and read a book.

After half an hour of running and playing, Emily called for her children to come eat. No one needed to be told twice, because all had worked up a healthy appetite. Emily spread the food on the blanket, as each of her children ran up to the picnic quilt. Even though Tim was closest to start out, he was the last to arrive. No one touched the food until Tim arrived and sat down, with Martha's help.

All the delicacies of a Cratchit family picnic were presented nicely on the quilt: homemade bread with freshly churned butter; dried fish and boiled potatoes, which had been diced and rubbed with basil; toasted bread, cubed and sprinkled with cinnamon sugar. "Mm-mmm, this looks delicious!" Robert proclaimed, and the family began to eat.

After a sip of water from his cup to wash down a bite of bread, Tim continued with his earlier thoughts, "But how, Father? How do we know?"

"Know what, Tim?" Robert asked, knowing Tim was always coming up with questions from someone twice his age.

"How do we know Grandmother is in Heaven?"

All other conversations between the Cratchits halted, as everyone focused their attention on Robert for the answer to Tim's question. Emily immediately began preparing her own version of an answer that defined faith, just in case Robert struggled with his response.

In a flash of remembrance from his childhood, Robert heard his father's last words spoken to him from his deathbed: *Butterflies are caterpillars that have been set free.* Now, with a clear and colorful vision, he understood his father's wisdom.

He stood and walked out of the shadow of the tree, and out into the open grass, as every eye followed him. The children glanced at one another, but no one spoke. At first, it seemed as though Robert walked away from the question, or maybe he was looking for an answer. After a few silent moments, he bent over and picked a flower. Then, he returned to his place on the quilt next to Emily.

Handing the flower to Tim, he asked, "Look, Tim, what do you see?"

Tim looked at the flower, then back to his father. "It has a caterpillar on it. A fuzzy little caterpillar, and he's eating the flower." The other children, even Martha, moved closer to Tim, in order to see the little caterpillar.

"That's right, my boy," Robert began, as the children returned their attention to him. "Now, consider the caterpillar. A loner, thinking only of himself and his constant appetite. Not able to see further than his next meal. Unable to understand the difference between this life and the next. No matter how many times you show him, he still sees only today, never tomorrow."

Robert leaned forward and lifted his hands, capturing everyone's attention as he continued. "Then, after a full caterpillar's life, he wraps himself in his blanket. He closes out the world, not really sure why he was there, or what he left in return for the abundance he so greedily consumed. All he has ever known was life as a caterpillar. Now it's over, with nothing to do now but sleep, never again to enjoy life as a caterpillar."

Robert focused his gaze directly into Tim's eyes. "Through the miracle of God's love, that poor little selfish, undeserving caterpillar transforms into a beautiful butterfly, full of life and color, riding the wind, free to explore a whole new world. No longer trapped in a clumsy laboring body, the butterfly flickers from flower to flower, feeding on nectar and dancing through the sky." He thrust his arms up and about as he spoke, imagining himself as the butterfly.

"Never has a butterfly wanted to turn back into a caterpillar. Nor has a caterpillar ever imagined that one day he would be a beautiful butterfly. This is God's promise to us. If He can perform this miracle, turning a caterpillar into a butterfly, then just imagine what He will do for us."

Tim looked back at the caterpillar on the flower, still in his hand, then back to his father. "Will I fly someday, Father?"

Robert looked to Emily, as tears pooled in his eyes. Emily took the lead and responded for him, "We all will, Tim. When the time is right, each in our own turn, we will soar with the angels. Do you understand what your father said, my love?"

"Yes, I think I do," Tim answered. "We know that Grandmother is in Heaven, because God shows us miracles every day to remind us how much He loves us."

"Well done, my boy," Robert responded, smiling at the son whose inquisitive nature and comprehension reminded him quite a lot of himself at his age. "Well done, indeed."

Chapter 23

At sixteen years old, Martha Cratchit, the first born of Robert and Emily Cratchit, was just as sweet and pretty as her mother, and every bit a Cratchit from the inside out. Martha was like a second mother around the home, caring for her siblings and assisting her mother with both the cooking and cleaning. It was a family decision, then, when she approached her parents with the idea of earning money outside the home.

As much as Emily had come to depend on Martha in recent years to help during the day, she understood as well that Martha was coming to an age when she would need to establish her own way in life. Martha's best friend, Trudy, introduced her to the foreman at the textile factory where she worked. With her obvious strong work ethic and glowing disposition, Martha secured a position as a seamstress, earning nearly two shillings a week.

At the end of each work day, it was not uncommon for Martha to stop at the market to buy some food for the family, particularly on payday. More often than not, she would contribute nearly all of her income to the family's welfare. Even though the work was hard, and her fingers often bled from working all day with the sewing needles, she never complained, at work or at home. Yes, every bit a Cratchit.

One night, Martha entered through the front door quietly, hoping to slip in unnoticed. Her father had arrived home a little earlier than normal and Emily was preparing dinner. Robert smiled as he saw his hardworking daughter step into the house, but dropped quickly into a state of concern as a feeling of dread swept over him. "Martha?"

"Good evening, Father." Robert watched as she tried to close the tear in her dress with her hands, but there was just too much damage for her to conceal the obvious.

Robert stood to examine his daughter more closely, as Emily joined him. "My dear, what happened?" he asked. "Are you alright?"

Martha immediately began trembling, as she reached out and embraced her mother. Even in the dimly lit room, Robert and Emily could tell she was hurt more than just her torn clothes. Emily put her hands on both sides of Martha's face and lifted her head until they made eye contact, "Martha, my dear, tell us."

All the way home, Martha dreaded talking to her parents and even imagined how she would walk through the room unnoticed to change her clothes. But looking directly into her mother's eyes, she lost the strength she thought she had to pretend she was unharmed, "Oh, Mother!" was all she could say before the tears began flowing. Robert quickly pulled two chairs next to Martha, so she and Emily could sit. He then pulled another chair up, and sat down beside her.

Emily held Martha close, as Robert held one of her hands. Both waited patiently for her to cry out her tears. After a few minutes, Martha lifted her face from her mother's shoulder and wiped her eyes. "I'm so sorry. I really didn't mean to bring my problems home."

"Tsk, my lamb," Robert said, trying to sooth her. "We share all that is good or bad. Please, go on."

Martha took a deep breath and then exhaled slowly. "I stopped at the market on the way home. You know, to buy some bread for dinner." Suddenly, she exclaimed. "Oh my! I lost the bread!"

Emily ran her fingers through Martha's tangled hair and pulled out some gravel and dirt. "Martha, please tell us. What happened to you?"

Noticing the scrapes on her hands and some blood on her elbow, Robert added, "Yes, Martha, please take your time."

She took another deep breath with her eyes closed and then opened them slowly. "When I was walking away from the market, a man came up from behind me and put his hand over my mouth, so that I couldn't scream. Then, he pulled me behind a wall."

Robert knew where this was heading and felt his heart drop into his stomach, unconsciously squeezing her hand tighter.

"He held me from behind as another man, who must have been keeping a lookout, came beside us. The man behind me put a knife against my throat and told me that if I screamed, it would be the last sound I ever made." She lifted her chin as she described the knife. Robert and Emily both saw the red line where a knife had pressed the skin enough to leave a scratch.

Tears formed in Robert's eyes, as he watched Emily pull her daughter into her arms, terrified of knowing the rest of the ordeal.

Martha continued, "The man beside me pulled on my dress, as the man behind me pushed me to the ground and punched me in the jaw."

Emily let out a whimper, and then quickly silenced herself so Martha could continue.

Looking into her mother's eyes, Martha cried out, "Oh Mother, they were going to rape me!"

Robert sat silently, as hatred filled his heart and a dark desire for revenge overtook his soul.

Martha stopped crying after a few moments, then looked at her father for the first time and smiled. As she wiped away the tears, she continued with a look of peace on her face. "And then a miracle happened." She turned her head to Emily and then back to Robert, to make sure they understood her. "Yes, a miracle is the only way I can describe it. The man with the knife was on top of me and the other had pulled my arms past my head, but suddenly the man holding my arms was gone. I didn't see what happened to him at first, but another man must have seen what was happening and hit that man with a board. Then he smashed the board straight into the face of the man with the knife. I think he broke his nose, for sure," she said with a nervous laugh.

Robert couldn't contain himself, jumping up and yelling, "Bravo!" Quickly, he regained control and sat back down next to Martha, anxious to hear the rest of her story, knowing the worst was surely over.

Relieved she had her parent's support, she went on, "This man was well dressed and all a gentleman, but he wasn't finished with my attackers. He went back to the first man and pounded him three times with his fist. I let out a scream, when I saw the knife man coming at him from behind. That must have warned him, because he turned and punched the man again on his broken nose. Well, after that, those two men took off running like rats on hot coals."

"Good Lord!" exclaimed Robert. "What a miracle, indeed!"

"Never mind that, Robert," Emily interrupted looking back to Martha. "Are you hurt, my dear?"

Robert followed his wife's lead. "Yes, Martha, are you alright?"

Martha managed a smile with a slight laugh of relief and nodded, "Yes, yes, I think I am."

"And do you know the man who helped you, my dear? I say I want to thank him with all my heart." Robert stood up, relieved the story ended with such a surprisingly good outcome. Emily went to the wash basin and returned to begin cleaning Martha's scrapes with a damp cloth.

"Well, the gentleman first helped me up and walked me out of the alley. He then said he had seen them grab me from across the street, where he'd been shopping with his wife. Even though it was dark, and there were two men to his one, he did not hesitate. I can't tell you how amazed I was that he did what he did!" Martha's face then lit up, as though she was finally recognizing the magnitude of his heroics. Continuing on, she said, "I walked with him across the street to where his wife was standing, and she immediately started brushing me off with her gloved hands. They both sat with me on a bench until I could stop shaking. When I asked the identity of the brave soul who risked his own safety for mine, he told me his name was Avery McFadden."

Hearing that name, Robert's knees weakened, as he slowly sat back down in his chair. He could barely hear Martha and Emily talking, as they went to another room to clean her wounds and change her clothes. *A miracle, indeed*, Robert thought, *more than any of them could know.* Robert's attention went inward to a memory from years before, and then he quickly saw all of the pieces fall into place, right before his eyes. *Avery McFadden was the son of Charles McFadden,* he recollected, *the boy I saved from the runaway horse when I myself was but a lad. An act of heroics begat another act of heroics.*

Indeed, the story his father had told him when he himself was a child, about sending ripples out through one's actions, had come back to him, in a perfectly clear way. He'd saved Avery, and Avery saved Martha. A shiver went through him at a most haunting thought: *Had I not dared to pursue that horse, how differently might this night have been had young Avery died that day? Who would have rescued my Martha?*

With a deeply grateful heart, Robert Cratchit whispered to himself just three words: "God in Heaven."

Chapter 24

Waking to the first snow of the season was always a welcome sight for both Robert and Emily Cratchit. When winter's white powder began to blanket the streets and rooftops, somehow it made, in the couple's eyes, an atmosphere of simplicity, beauty and tranquility. They both knew it would not be long before the ash and soot from thousands of coal-burning fires throughout London deposited a dark film over the virgin snow—so they'd relish that first falling all the more.

One such wintery morning, Robert woke to find Emily's side of the bed empty. He arose to see if she needed help stoking the fire, but he soon realized she was nowhere in the home. He opened the door to the bright white of the sun reflecting off of the snow, which nearly blinded him. As he stood there with his eyes adjusting, without warning, he felt the impact directly on his chest—the first snowball of the season being flung at him!

Emily stood just a few steps away, pointing and laughing at the startled look on his face. He stooped down and quickly gathered two handfuls of snow and chased after the woman who, he knew, wanted to be caught. Emily stopped in her tracks and turned to face Robert, who was now only a couple of paces behind her, which allowed him to collide with her as she wrapped her arms around him and pressed the side of her face to his chest for warmth. Robert tossed the snow he carried above them, adding to the snow that had already fallen on them. Emily asked, "Don't you just love the first snow?"

Robert kissed his wife, still panting from the run in the brisk morning air, and then replied, "Not nearly as much as I love you." They stood alone, embracing in the street, as the stillness of the early morning snow brought a quiet reverence to the couple, who treasured the moment. "Christmas is coming," Robert said as though their short, but fun, skirmish in the snow trumpeted the season.

Walking to work through the snow was often a slippery ordeal, so Robert left home earlier than normal. What made the trek even longer were the distractions brought on by boys with snowballs who took aim at the top hats of men on the street. Robert playfully returned the snowballs aimed at *his* top hat, until the boys would find a less suspecting target.

As Robert continued making his way to the office, one snow-sloshing step after another, the words "Save the cat!" came from the familiar ghostly voice of Jacob Marley. As he walked along the very next block, Robert spied a kitten curled up against the bricks of a building. He picked up the kitten, but believed he was too late, as it felt stiff, probably frozen. Still, he complied with Jacob's request and tucked the frozen creature inside his coat, while he kept an eye out for a different, "livelier" cat that may have stood a better chance for survival.

However, by the time he unlocked the door to the office, Robert detected slight movements from the kitten inside his coat, as it lay next to his heart for warmth. Once he lit the coal burner, the kitten was breathing regularly, although still listless.

Robert kept the kitten in his lap as he started warming his inkwell, even after Scrooge entered the office. He had to look away to control his urge to laugh, as he watched Scrooge brush the snow from his hat and press the dent that had been created by the obvious impact of a well-aimed snowball. He was thankful, as well, that he could not understand the words Scrooge mumbled, which were most certainly intended for the boys who pelted him with snow.

When Robert needed to leave his desk, he would set the quiet kitten in his chair, and then pick it up to hold again after he returned. As the morning progressed, the kitten's condition improved and by noon, it was all Robert could do to contain the kitten and appear undistracted to Scrooge's watchful eye.

After several cries for food from the kitten, Robert noticed Scrooge return his quill to its holder and listen intently. Scrooge walked from his desk into the outer room where Robert worked and inquired, "Cratchit, do you hear something?"

Robert did not need to respond, as the kitten once again cried out, this time to the sound of Scrooge's voice. Robert slowly lifted the kitten from his lap for Scrooge to see, and immediately began pleading his case. "I found him, sir, frozen in the snow on my way here this morning. Please, sir, he will be no bother and I will take him home at the end of the day."

To be mean, for meanness' sake, Scrooge grabbed the kitten from Robert's hands and yelled while he walked, "I am not here to take in strays! I am running a business, sir, a fact of which you should be well aware!"

Opening the door, Scrooge tossed the kitten to the street and slammed the door behind it. Robert lost control of his emotions and in a rare outburst stood to challenge his employer. "Mr. Scrooge! He will die out there!"

As Robert made his way to the same door with the intent to retrieve the kitten, Scrooge grabbed his walking stick and pointed the silver grip toward him, lashing back, "Mr. Cratchit, I do not pay you to rescue strays, nor do I allow filthy animals in my office! If you leave to get that cat, then take it home and find yourself another place to work and live!"

Robert promptly made his way to the front window, but stopped short of exiting through the door. From the window, he saw the kitten in the street and watched as a well-dressed woman, carrying a parasol to block the falling snow, accompanied by a small child, stopped to pick the kitten up from the street and hand it to her daughter, who held it tenderly in her arms.

"Cratchit!" Scrooge called out, making Robert's whole body jump. Still, he continued to watch as the pair walked away with the kitten, his boss's words echoing behind him. "Back to work, sir, while you still have your position!"

Robert did as ordered, angry and disgusted with this man who was so callous that he would throw a sick kitten out into the snow to die. It did, however, relieve him to know the kitten had been rescued for the *second* time in one day. Jacob Marley never explained the ripples that were sure to follow when Robert did as he was instructed, but he *had* learned, over the years, there were always consequences to his actions.

Sitting back down at his desk, Robert began reflecting upon what had just transpired. *When Marley was alive, only sorrow and pain followed his arduous acts of ill intent. But in death, although I rarely seem to understand the intent of his instructions, joy and happiness spread far beyond my comprehension.*

With Christmas just a few weeks away, Robert found his attention drifting to the Christmas Day festivities so evident in the community around him. Street vendors stood in the snow selling roasted chestnuts and hot broth. Songs of the holiday season filled the air, while more often than not; strangers and passersby greeted one another with kindhearted pleasantries. All of these changes buoyed his spirit, as he worked hard one evening to finish up and get back home to his family.

Just before Robert locked the office, after Scrooge had left for the day, Fred Holloway walked through the door to find Robert fastening his coat. "Mr. Holloway," Robert exclaimed, as he turned to see his friend.

"Robert Cratchit," Fred replied, offering him a hearty handshake. "Still having trouble calling me Fred, I see."

Both men laughed together, as Robert corrected himself. "Fred, how are you, sir? I'm sorry, but you just missed your uncle."

"Which is why I come at this hour, Robert. I've only the stomach to see him but once a year, and that day is still weeks away."

"Well, please," Robert said, motioning for Fred to step into the office, "come in and tell me how I may serve you."

The men both hung their coats and sat by the remaining embers still smoldering in the stove. "How are your wife and children?" Robert started, enjoying the fact that Fred now had children to brag on.

"All well and good, Robert. Allie is a peach and knows just how to get what she wants from her father, and Adam wears me out with his games and sport."

"Oh, how wonderful to hear, sir." Robert couldn't seem to stop smiling in Fred's company.

"And how is the Cratchit family fairing?"

"All quite well, sir, thank you. My eldest, Martha, is working as a skilled seamstress. And all of my children are reading and writing, thanks to their school masters, and the teaching skills of my good wife."

"Excellent! And you know, that actually brings me to the purpose of my visit this evening. I wanted to catch you before you left to ask you about your eldest son."

"Ah, Peter."

"Yes, Peter. Do you think Peter is prepared to assume his place in the working world? You see, I have a position opening in my company for an apprenticeship."

"Oh my, yes! Yes, indeed! Peter is seventeen years old and very mature."

"Good! That is wonderful. I told my wife that if Robert Cratchit's son was half the man of his father, he would be a rare find for our business."

"Oh sir, it is *you* who do me the honor. I cannot imagine a finer man for whom Peter can work."

"Now I can only pay him five shillings and six pence to start, but if he is truly his father's son, he will move up quickly and I will find myself answering to him one day." Fred smiled and again Robert felt he was in the presence of joy itself. "Do me a favor and don't announce this to Peter until Christmas. Have him come to my office the first day of the New Year and we will get him started."

"I shall indeed, sir. Thank you, thank you, Fred."

The men dressed to go to their respective homes, but Fred asked one more question before their final handshake. "How *is* my uncle these days, Robert?"

"Very much the same as in years past. He seems very lonely, if you ask me, but it is by his own choosing that he is so. I dare say that without Mr. Marley these last seven years, no one would step forward and claim to be his friend."

"Seven years, already. Hm-m. . . Well, cheer up, Robert. I will come on Christmas Eve and invite him to Christmas dinner. It seems to give him great pleasure to chastise and reject me." Fred gave Robert a wink and a pat on his shoulder.

Robert smiled and replied, "Whether you know it or not, I look forward to that every year, Fred."

Chapter 25

As promised, after the noon hour on Christmas Eve, Fred entered his uncle's office as quiet as a church mouse. Robert approached him at the door to help him hang his coat, scarf, and hat with not a word spoken between them.

"Merry Christmas, Uncle!" Fred called out in a cheerful voice, coming upon Scrooge so quickly that he was briefly startled by his nephew's approach.

"Bah!" replied Scrooge. "Humbug!"

"Christmas a humbug, Uncle? You don't mean that, I'm sure."

"I do," said Scrooge. "*Merry* Christmas? What right have you to be merry? What reason have you to be merry? You're poor enough."

"Come, then," returned Fred. "What right have you to be dismal? What reason have you to be miserable? You're rich enough."

Scrooge, having no better answer ready on the spur of the moment, said "Bah!" again, and followed it up once more with "Humbug!"

"Don't be cross, Uncle!"

"What else can I be, when I live in such a world of fools as this? *Merry Christmas?* What's Christmas time to you but a time for paying bills without money, a time for finding yourself a year older, but not an hour richer? If I had my way," said Scrooge indignantly, "every idiot who goes about with 'Merry Christmas' on his lips should be boiled with his own pudding and buried with a stake of holly through his heart!"

"Uncle!" pleaded Fred.

"Nephew!" replied Scrooge, sternly. "Keep Christmas in your own way, and let me keep it in mine."

"Keep it? But you don't keep it."

"Let me leave it alone, then. Much good may it do you! Much good it has ever done you!"

Robert listened intently from his desk, as the two men bantered their points rather loudly. In all of his years in the presence of Scrooge, he had never known anyone, even Jacob Marley himself, to challenge Scrooge as bravely as Fred Holloway did this Christmas Eve. So riveting was Fred's debate with his uncle that Robert found himself gesturing cheers for the hero of what seemed a well scripted play, in which Scrooge was cast perfectly as the villain.

At that moment, Robert could hear Fred's quiet strength rise up even more so in his voice. "There are many things from which I might have derived good, but by which I have not profited, I dare say. Christmas is among them. I am sure I have always thought of Christmas time as a good time—a kind, forgiving, charitable, pleasant time—the only time I know of, in the long calendar of the year, when men and women think of people below them as if they really were fellow passengers on a common path, and not just another race of creatures bound on other journeys. And therefore, Uncle, though it has never put a scrap of gold or silver in my pocket, I believe it has done me good, and will do me good. And so I say, God bless it!"

Robert, seated at his desk, involuntarily began applauding, before reality reminded him he was siding against his own employer. Taking heed of this impropriety, he quickly busied himself with his work, diverting his attention from the private conversation in Scrooge's office.

"Let me hear another sound from you," said Scrooge, pointing the silver grip of his walking stick at Robert, "and you'll keep your Christmas by losing your position here!" Turning back to Fred, he added, "You're quite a powerful speaker, sir. I wonder why you don't go into Parliament."

"Don't be angry, Uncle. Come! Dine with us tomorrow."

"I cannot." Then Scrooge clarified himself. "I will not, Nephew."

"But why?" implored Fred. "Why?"

A chill swept through the office, as Fred, a most charming and convincing fellow to most who knew him, had failed to thaw the icy heart of his uncle. Even the flame from the single candle on Robert's desk offered no warmth. He moved to the coal burner that rested between his desk and Scrooge's office to stir the embers of the fire, but with no fuel remaining in the burnt ash, the last ember extinguished. Robert contemplated adding a brick of coal to the burner for a brief moment, but he could feel Scrooge's eyes following him.

"Good afternoon," said Scrooge in an attempt to end what he considered a most unpleasant conversation.

"I want nothing from you," Fred replied. "I ask nothing of you. Why can we not be friends?"

"Good afternoon," said Scrooge, louder than before, wanting nothing more to do with his nephew's intrusion on his day.

"I am sorry, with all my heart, to find you so resolute. We have never had any quarrel, to which I have been a party. But I have made my best try in homage to Christmas, and I'll keep my Christmas humor to the last. So a Merry Christmas, Uncle!"

"Good afternoon," said Scrooge.

"And a Happy New Year!"

"Good afternoon!" yelled Scrooge.

Fred retreated from Scrooge's office without an angry word. He stopped at the outer door to wish the greetings of the season on Robert, who, cold as he was, was warmer than Scrooge, for he returned them cordially.

"There's another fellow," muttered Scrooge, who overheard Robert's reply to Fred. "My clerk, with fifteen shillings a week, and a wife and family, talking about a Merry Christmas. I am alone in my sanity."

Robert stood to help Fred with his coat and scarf. "I'm sorry, Fred," he said in a hushed voice, "for Mr. Scrooge's feelings toward you. But I must say, sir, that your speech gets better with every passing year. I most enjoy your appreciation for Christmas and the good you see in others. Indeed I do, sir."

Fred smiled with the warmth of the season, as he tilted his freshly donned hat at his longtime friend. "It's all good, Robert. I will not let his despair darken my day. To the contrary, I feel energized after standing up to such a sorrowful soul. I believe I shall go buy my children a gift and wish a Merry Christmas to a hundred people before returning home, beginning with you, my friend. Merry Christmas Robert, to you and your family."

"Oh thank you, sir, and a very Merry Christmas to you and your lovely family, as well."

While letting Fred out, Robert let two other people in. They were portly gentlemen, pleasant to behold, and now stood, with their hats off, in Scrooge's office. They had books and papers in their hands, and while facing Scrooge at his desk, bowed to him.

"Scrooge and Marley's, I believe," said one of the gentlemen, referring to his list. "Have I the pleasure of addressing Mr. Scrooge or Mr. Marley?"

"Mr. Marley has been dead these seven years," Scrooge replied. "He died seven years ago, this very night."

"We have no doubt his liberality is well represented by his surviving partner," said one of the gentlemen, presenting his credentials to Scrooge.

The lack of it certainly was, thought Robert, *for while Marley was alive, both men had been two kindred spirits.* At the ominous word 'liberality,' Scrooge frowned, shook his head, and handed the credentials back.

"At this festive season of the year, Mr. Scrooge," said the gentleman, taking up a pen, "it is more than usually desirable that we should make some slight provision for the poor and destitute, who suffer greatly at the present time. Many thousands are in want of common necessaries. Hundreds of thousands are in want of common comforts, sir."

"Are there no prisons?" asked Scrooge.

"Plenty of prisons," said the gentleman, laying down the pen again."

"And the Union workhouses?" demanded Scrooge. "Are they still in operation?"

"They are. Still," returned the gentleman, "I wish I could say they were not."

"The Treadmill and the Poor Law are in full vigor, then?"

"Both very busy, sir."

"Oh! I was afraid, from what you said at first, that something had occurred to stop them in their useful course. I'm very glad to hear it," Scrooge responded with sarcastic overtones.

While overhearing the conversation between Scrooge and the two gentlemen, Robert thought back on his childhood, to the fate of his own father, who was sent to debtor's prison by Scrooge for failing to fully compensate Scrooge and Marley for back rent. After all of these years, the wound was still deep.

"Nothing!" Scrooge replied. Hearing Scrooge's voice raise toward the gentlemen brought Robert's attention back to their conversation.

"You wish to be anonymous?"

"I wish to be left alone. Since you ask me what I wish, gentlemen, that is my answer. I don't make merry myself at Christmas and I can't afford to make idle people merry. I help to support the establishments I have mentioned. They cost enough, and those who are badly off must go there."

"Many can't go there, and many would rather die."

"If they would rather die, they had better do it, and decrease the surplus population."

Robert knew he could do nothing against his employer in retaliation, nor punish him with revenge. However, to hear him describe the poor, such as his own father must have been to Scrooge, as 'surplus' stirred a measure of anger within Robert's soul that he had not felt in a very long time.

"It's not my business," Scrooge added. "It's enough for a man to understand his own business, and not to interfere with other people's. Mine occupies me constantly. Good afternoon, gentlemen!"

Seeing clearly that it would be useless to pursue their point, the gentlemen withdrew and Scrooge returned to his work.

Chapter 26

"You'll want all day tomorrow, I suppose?" said Scrooge.

"If it's convenient, sir," replied Robert, hopeful that Fred's visit and the charitable gentlemen had not soured Scrooge's mood to the point of forcing him to work on Christmas day.

"It's not convenient," said Scrooge, "and it's not fair. If I was not to pay your wages for a day, you'd think yourself mistreated, wouldn't you?"

Robert smiled faintly.

"And yet," said Scrooge, "you don't think *I'm* being mistreated when I pay you a day's wages for *no work*."

"It's only once a year, sir," Robert humbly observed.

"A poor excuse for picking a man's pocket every twenty-fifth of December!" Scrooge griped, buttoning his greatcoat to the chin. "But I suppose you must have the whole day. Be here all the earlier the next morning."

"I will sir, and thank you, Mr. Scrooge."

After Scrooge walked out with a growl, Robert quickly closed the office. With the long ends of his white knitted scarf dangling below his waist (for he boasted no greatcoat), he briskly walked toward Camden Town, where his family anticipated his return.

Before entering a poultry shop to buy a goose for Christmas dinner, Robert stopped to notice the prize turkey, proudly displayed in the front window, suspended by its feet. *Enough to feed a village,* Robert thought to himself, amazed any bird could have grown so large.

A warm sense of peace and tranquility filled Robert to his very soul, such a sensation that comes over a person when he strives to serve his fellow man with goodwill. The feeling one gets when in the presence of divine love.

"My time here has nearly ended," Robert heard someone say behind him. Instinctively turning to see who it was, he spun completely around before realizing he recognized the sound as that of Jacob Marley's spirit.

"Through your service and grace," Marley continued, "I have amended the sins of my past. I have but one more deed to perform, but this one I must do on my own this very night. Farewell, my friend."

And with that, Jacob Marley detached from Robert Cratchit, but stayed just long enough to hear Robert wish him well. "God bless you, Jacob Marley," Robert said aloud, unconcerned if any passersby heard him speaking alone to the night sky. "And Merry Christmas, my friend."

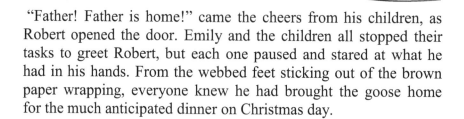

"Father! Father is home!" came the cheers from his children, as Robert opened the door. Emily and the children all stopped their tasks to greet Robert, but each one paused and stared at what he had in his hands. From the webbed feet sticking out of the brown paper wrapping, everyone knew he had brought the goose home for the much anticipated dinner on Christmas day.

Robert laid the goose on the table and the children watched, as Emily carefully removed the brown paper wrapping. Then, as if by signal, everyone touched the feathers and remarked on the softness.

"Now, now," started Emily, "I promised Belinda this would be her year to pluck the goose." Each of the Cratchit children congratulated Belinda for it being her turn to do the most prestigious chore available on Christmas Eve.

As Belinda studied the goose, the rest of the family quickly returned to their work at hand. So much was needed to prepare for a festive Christmas in the Cratchit household, and everyone had a role to play. Peter cracked walnuts, meticulously separating nut from shell, while Martha scrubbed the wooden floor. Cleaning out the fireplace was delegated to Tim, whose approach to the chore often entertained his siblings—regularly enough, he would get more coal ash on his face and hands than in the bucket!

After resting from his walk home and warming himself by the fire, Robert asked his family, "Who would like to accompany me to church this Christmas Eve to light a candle for our saints?"

"I would like to go with you, Father," came the singular voice of Tiny Tim.

Hearing no other volunteers, Robert stood to address Tim, "Then it shall be just you and me, Tim, as everyone else is working hard to serve the hardest working woman in London."

As she blushed at the compliment, Emily mentioned to her husband, "Bundle Tim up well, Robert. We don't want him to catch cold, I dare say."

As instructed, Tim was wrapped from head to toe in several layers of clothing, before being hoisted to his father's shoulder with crutch in hand. With a farewell kiss for his wife, they headed for the door. "Off we go. We shan't be long, my dears."

The other children waved goodbye, quietly appreciating the glow on Tim's face, as he sat high on his father's shoulder.

Upon entering the front of the church, Robert lowered Tim to the ground. He first removed his own hat and then Tim's. Robert walked slowly alongside Tim, as they made their way down the center aisle of the church. Tim struggled to keep pace, though, since he walked with the added burden of winter clothes between him and his small wooden crutch.

There was no service scheduled, but a number of the faithful sat quietly in thought and prayer, scattered throughout the pews. All eyes were on Tiny Tim, who labored with each passing step, and his father, who walked patiently and proudly next to his son.

At the end of the aisle, the altar was lined with candles, some lit and some not. When they reached the altar, Robert knelt, as did Tim beside him. Picking up a wooden stick with a burnt end, Robert lit it from a burning candle, then proceeded to light a candle of his own. Instead of snuffing the lit stick, he handed it to Tim, who lit the candle next to his father's, and then handed the lit stick back to his father, who extinguished the flame and laid three coins between the candles.

Heads bowed and hands clasped while on bended knee, the two Cratchits reverently entered into silent prayer. A few minutes passed before Robert and Tim stood together and made their way back down the same aisle from which they entered. Now, Tim saw the eyes that had previously followed him, each rewarded with his precious smile.

Before exiting the church, Robert knelt next to Tim to bundle him up in preparation for the trip home in the freezing weather. "Father?" Tim asked, "who did you pray for?"

"Why, I prayed for my own father, my mother, my sister, my wife and my children. Who did you pray for, Tim?"

"Well, I prayed for my family, and," he paused, as if unsure if he should go on, then finished, "and I prayed for Mr. Scrooge."

Robert instantly stopped fastening the clasps on Tim's coat and asked, "What in the world enticed you to pray for Mr. Scrooge?"

"I don't know, really. I just felt like he needed a prayer tonight. I prayed that somehow, his heart would be filled with the Spirit of Christmas."

Robert looked in Tim's eyes, realizing he was gazing into the soul of a boy who must surely be one of Heaven's favorites.

A moment later, Tim asked, "Father, do you see the way people look at me when I walk by them?"

"Yes, I do, Tim. Does it bother you?"

"No, not at all, Father. I hope when people see me, they'll remember the one who made lame people walk and blind people see."

Robert suddenly became so overwhelmed with emotion that he realized he could not leave the church just yet. "Tim, can you wait right here for me? I have something more that I must do before we go home."

Robert hurried back down the aisle toward the altar, this time with tears streaming down his cheeks. Dropping to his knees, he engaged in the deepest, most meaningful prayer of his life.

Please, please, spare the life of my Tiny Tim. If anyone must die, I pray that it will be me, for I am but a shadow of the man that Tim will be.

That evening, when all the Cratchit's gathered about the fire, each member of the family took a turn singing their favorite carol or hymn. This simple, yet rich tradition of theirs was a way of filling their Christmas Eve with good will and glad tidings. Yet, an overwhelming sadness brought sorrow to Robert's heart, as he quietly studied his young, crippled son. He watched Tiny Tim struggle for each breath, as he began a new verse of "God Rest Ye Merry Gentlemen." The dark rings around his eyes, which sank back into such a feeble young face, reinforced Robert's feelings that this may, indeed, be the last Christmas they would share. This coming year, he feared he would bury his son and somehow muster the strength to carry on.

Later that night, when the carolers were quiet and the children asleep, Robert pulled a chair next to Emily in front of the fire and confided his fears, finally speaking the words they had both held back from acknowledging to each other. "I just don't know how to save him, Emily. So many times I have fought, quite successfully I might add, to help the needy. But now, when my own son needs me, I'm powerless. I pray on this Christmas, that God will grace our family with his blessings."

"Oh, Robert!" Emily said, trying to console him as much as herself. "You may help the homeless, but only God chooses who among us shall live or die. If He takes Tim from us, it will be to ease his suffering and to reward such a good soul with eternal love. It will not be to punish us."

Emily had more to say, as she had rehearsed this speech for many quiet evenings in front of the fire. But when she brought herself to look into Robert's tearful eyes and saw his chin quivering as he fought back his fears, she lost her own controls and fell against his shoulder weeping. No more was said, until there were no more tears to fall.

"When I was a boy," Robert began, "not much older than Tim, I asked my father if we were poor. I truly understand now what he told me then. I have never achieved riches or fame, but indeed, as I look around, I am surrounded by great wealth. It is clear to me now that a man's wealth is measured by the love one shares, and I share the love of a beautiful wife and the finest family in London."

Emily raised her head just enough to kiss her husband on the cheek, before resting once again on his shoulder and adding her own thoughts on the matter. "True, my love, but your wealth is also measured in the lives you selflessly touch. Most every corner of this city knows of your selfless acts of kindness and deeds. Every time you serve one of God's children, you serve Him, as well."

"Come, my love," Robert urged his wife, as he tried to change the mood, lightly squeezing her arm. "We should get some rest, ourselves, as we have a big day tomorrow. I can barely wait to enjoy your Christmas feast. I dare say I won't sleep a wink tonight, for fear I'll sleep through the meal and miss your marvelous cooking." With that, Emily raised her head from his tear-soaked shoulder and gave him a smile that said 'I do' all over again.

Chapter 27

Indeed, sleep *was* difficult for Robert to find, as he lay in bed next to Emily. He listened for long minutes, as her breathing became rhythmic. He knew she had found her way to a peaceful slumber, but for him, the flurry of so many images and ideas in his head would not let him rest. Memories of Christmases long past and expectations of the Christmas nearly upon them filled his thoughts.

With his eyes open now, Robert stared up at the ceiling and listened to all sorts of noises and sounds wafting in and out in the still of the night. An alley cat chasing a mouse. A man walking down the street singing his own drunken version of, coincidentally, "God Rest Ye Merry Gentlemen." A horse pulling a cart with a slow and steady cadence of clip-clop, its hooves stepping heavily along the cobblestone street.

He tried again to close his eyes and clear his mind, but quickly opened them when a light shown around all four sides of the door to their room, making the door appear as though it was un-tethered to the frame. He looked quickly to Emily to ask her if she knew why there was a light coming from the next room, but decided to investigate without disturbing her sleep.

As he opened the door, the light that was framing it now bathed him with warmth. Paradoxically, the light was brighter than any he had seen before, yet it was pleasant to his eyes. Instead of the wooden table, chairs, and fireplace he expected to see when he opened the door, he found himself standing at the top of a lighthouse, which was the source of the radiating light. Suddenly, the door through which he walked was gone, and he was looking out to sea.

On his left, his father, Peter, stood beside him, and on his right, his mother, Becky. His mother smiled at him, her face glowing as brightly as the love he felt from her, yet she did not speak. Peter was not the frail, battered shell of a man as he was when Robert last saw him alive. Instead, he was the strong, burly coal miner he knew as a child. "Father?" Robert asked, confused as to how he could have gone from a sleepless night to this transcendent moment between time and space.

With a voice that seemed to echo from the clouds above the ocean, Peter responded, "Here you will find the answer to your prayers, my son. Look, Robert, look upon the water. Tell me what you see."

Gazing out as far as he could see, Robert saw nothing but the ocean. Then, a feeling of deep peace came over him, as he realized the answer to his father's question, "The waves, Father. The ripples in the sea. They come back to me."

With that, Robert closed his eyes. Basking in the all-embracing warmth of the lighthouse, he felt the unconditional love from his parents on either side of him and cherished this moment that would be with him forever. With eyes shut, he felt the arms of his sister Lizzy wrap around his waist from behind, just as she had done years ago when he first laid eyes on baby Martha. He did not see his sister, but her presence was instantly recognizable.

Robert then realized he must have a hundred questions for his parents, but slowly opening his eyes, he saw only darkness. The sounds of the ocean waves crashing upon the shore were replaced by a neighbor pouring a bucket of water on the cobblestone walk just outside. The light faded into the dimly lit streetlamp just past his window. The arm across his waist was Emily's, as she held him close for warmth on this cold winter's night. But the feelings he'd felt were still in his heart. He didn't jump up from bed in a panic. He wasn't knocked unconscious. He just had a warm, knowing sense of reassurance inside that conveyed to him, *everything will be fine now.* Kissing his sleeping wife on her cheek, Robert drifted off to his own restful state, thinking about how marvelous Christmas morning would be with his family.

The quiet dawn was broken by the sounds of church bells announcing Christmas day. Robert sat up in bed and smiled, remembering the Christmas Eve "visit" he'd just had with his parents and sister. Emily was the first one up, cleaning vegetables and preparing a fire. Where coal normally burned on the frigid winter days in London, today's fire would be consuming wood Robert had been collecting for months. Each Cratchit would take turns cranking the goose over a slow-burning fire. The reward would be a succulent bird, crisp on the outside, tender and juicy within.

"Merry Christmas, my love," were Robert's first words, nearly sung with enthusiasm as he greeted his wife.

"Merry Christmas," Emily responded, hesitating a moment to look deep into the eyes of the man she loved. Preparing the Christmas meal would be an all-day event that required careful planning and timing. She'd been reviewing the steps over and over in her mind, all the way through to the making of the plum pudding. And although her pudding was always a masterpiece of perfection, still she fretted as though it was her first attempt.

One by one, the Cratchits woke with a cheerful Christmas greeting and a verse or two from a seasonal carol. When one would start up a Christmas song, others would join in. Every Cratchit, both big and small, began helping out with the Christmas morning chores. Emily stopped, turned completely around for a quick survey of the room, and declared, "There now, I believe I am ready to start!" Everyone laughed at Emily's jovial mood.

"But first, my dear," Robert interrupted.

"Yes, first, children," Emily picked up on her cue. "Gather around the fire." Martha was rotating the goose, while everyone pulled a chair close to the fire and watched, as the heat from the burning logs made the skin on the bird sizzle.

Robert sat amongst his loving family and opened the family Bible to the Book of Mathew, and began reading the Nativity to the family. "And it came to pass in those days, that there went out a decree from Caesar Augustus, that all the world should be taxed..."

Emily and all the Cratchit children sat attentively listening, as Robert's reading brought the story to life. Just outside the window, snow fell silently, as though providing a reverent backdrop for this Christmas morning. When Robert finished and closed the Bible, everyone applauded his reading, as though they had just enjoyed a street performer.

"And now, my dears," Robert continued, "your mother and I have a gift for each of you." Again, applause broke out with cheers. Emily ran off to her bed and, from under it, pulled out five packages, each wrapped with brown paper and tied with string.

"I must admit, it isn't much," she said, returning with the packages.

All five children disputed her humble approach. "Oh, Mother, don't be silly!" All eyes were on the packages, wondering which was their own. With no markings, no one could understand how she knew which package went to each of them.

"Martha, my eldest, yours will be first." Emily extended a package to Martha. Peter stood up, in order to take over the cranking of the goose, giving his seat to Martha.

She untied the string and handed it to her mother, who would save it for the next year. With a childlike smile on her face and a glance around the room to see that all of her siblings were watching her, Martha carefully unfolded the paper wrapping to reveal a dainty kerchief that was hand embroidered by her mother. She held it up for all to see, while her mouth opened, searching for words of thanks. "Oh, Mother, oh Father, how exquisite! I love it so much! Thank you!"

She stood and leaned forward to hug her mother and father, each in their own turn. Emily breathed a sigh of relief, concerned for days her daughter might not appreciate the effort. As a seamstress, Martha was most impressed with the needlework she understood had taken her mother many hours of delicate stitching.

Next, Peter got everyone's attention by exchanging places with Martha once again, so as to receive *his* gift. Excitedly opening his package, Peter revealed to all an adult gentleman's collar. It didn't matter to him at all that it was the same collar he had seen on his father on many occasions. Peter held it in his hands with deep appreciation, as he understood this to be his parent's way of acknowledging him as a grown gentleman, preparing to take his own place in the world. "Thank you, Father. Thank you, Mother. I shall wear it proudly." He then got up and gave each of them a grateful hug.

Turning to the entire family, Robert then announced, "Well, Peter, I have something more for you, something for which I have held my tongue for weeks, waiting for this very moment."

All eyes were on their father, especially Peter's as Robert basked in the dramatic pause that was broken by his children asking in unison, "What, Father? What is it?"

"For my eldest son, Master Peter," he continued, "he will wear his gentleman's collar on his first day of work. I have my eye on a position that will net him a full five shillings and six pence per week."

Peter's eyes grew wide with excitement about this news. His siblings each congratulated him with a pat on the back. "You'll be quite the gentleman about town now, Peter," Martha declared.

Robert glanced at Emily, who was watching her son become a man, right before her eyes. Together, they shared the same thought, *First Martha, and now Peter. They're growing up so fast.*

Belinda opened a package that was a well-mended lavender dress Martha once wore when she was fourteen. Richard was happy to open the blue and grey wool hat and scarf, which Emily had knitted.

"And last, but certainly not least, for Tiny Tim," Robert said, as he handed Tim his gift.

Tim held the package, wanting the moment to last forever. He looked at each person in the room and grinned.

"Well go on, Tim, open it!" Richard shouted, encouraging him to reveal the secret inside the wrapped package. Tim slowly pulled the string loose and paused again, noticing all eyes were on him, encouraging him to keep going.

Little by little, Tim pulled the paper back, until he could no longer pace himself, finally flinging the brown paper to the floor. "It's, it's, a- . . ."

"Well, what is it, Tim?" Martha asked, while slowly turning the goose.

Tim held up high, for all to see, a wooden carved horse on rockers. The horse was perched on a block that connected it to the rockers, and the legs were pinned so they could move back and forth. Tim sat the little rocking horse on the table beside him and started it rocking. While in motion, the legs swung back and forth, striking the center perch. Each leg was carved in a position that made the horse appear to be running. When the legs struck the perch, they made a repeating clippity-clop sound, just like the sounds a horse makes on cobblestone streets.

But to Tim, the sound brought a different meaning, "Oh, Father! It's just like the sounds you make when I ride on your shoulders. It's like magic!"

Everyone loved Tim's animated enthusiasm. His laugh was contagious, and within seconds, every Cratchit was taking a turn rocking the horse and listening to the clippity-clop. Robert was especially heartened to see his son's face radiating so much joy. *I can hardly wait*, Robert thought, *to tell Mr. Knight about the gladness he's brought to Tiny Tim's Christmas. I dare say he could make a good living as a toymaker, if he ever tires of making pipes.*

Suddenly, they all heard a knock on the door. "I wonder who that is on this fine Christmas day," Robert said, as he leaped from his chair and approached the door. To his surprise, he greeted a portly round gentleman holding a turkey by the feet that was nearly half his size.

"Robert Cratchit?" the man inquired.

"Yes, yes, I'm Robert Cratchit, but what- . . ."

"This 'ere is for you, Mr. Cratchit. A gift, it is—a gift from an anonymous donor."

Robert took the bird by the feet, speechless for a moment, as the weight of the bird pulled his arm to the ground.

"For me? Are you sure? See here, my fine fellow, who is it from?"

As the poulterer climbed back up into the seat of his buggy, he laughed and said, "'He wouldn't be anonymous if you knew his name now, would he!"

The Cratchit family slowly circled Robert and the enormous turkey, which was plump with white and black feathers. "Who would do such a thing?" Emily asked, knowing there was no answer coming to her question. "Can we keep it, Robert?"

Robert's mind raced, matching names with faces from anyone who might have wanted to give his family such a gift. *"It's probably Mr. McFadden,"* he thought, *"but I can't be certain."*

Just then, Tim raised his voice, standing there with his crutch under one arm and his wooden horse under the other. "I think I know who sent it."

"Who?" Robert replied.

"Mr. Scrooge," Tim said confidently.

Most of the Cratchits laughed in response to Tim's answer, as if he had just told a good joke. Robert, however, pressed him further. "Tsk, tsk, Tim, what on earth would make you think of Mr. Scrooge?"

"I don't know, really. I just think it."

Robert looked at Emily. "Keep it," he said. "Clean it, stuff it, and cook it, my love. Tonight, the Cratchit household will be serving up a feast, the likes of which Camden Town has never witnessed!"

Everyone cheered, as Robert flung the huge bird on the table. As he knew the goose rotating over the fire was enough for each family member to have a good-sized serving with their Christmas meal, *but* that it was not possible for the five of them to consume both the goose *and* such a large turkey, he turned to his eldest son and said, "Peter, go about the building and tell all of our friends and neighbors that tonight at seven sharp, the Cratchit's will be serving turkey to all who hunger for some. Oh, and invite them to bring their favorite dish to share with others, as well. By God, we are going to have a banquet!"

Peter did as he was asked, and before long, the word went out to all who dwelled in the building, and then it spread to others, as well. Soon, both birds were sharing the same spit, rotating over a fire that burned all day. People came to the Cratchit's just to see the turkey they'd heard word about from this or that neighbor. Furniture was rearranged, as tables were set up and neighbors' chairs were brought in. Throughout the day, people came by to set a dish on the table, or bring a bottle of homemade wine, or to contribute a piece of wood for the fire. Women ran from home to home, sharing and borrowing ingredients for their specialty dishes.

At seven o'clock, as promised, the feast began. People were lined out the door with their plates and bowls. Somehow, there was more food than people, even though they kept coming. A couple of men stood near the fire playing Christmas songs on their fiddles, while people sang and danced around the crowded main room. Robert stood in awe of the sight, as he pulled Peter to his side, doing as his father had once done for him. "You see, Peter? Do you see how much joy the generosity of one man can bring? One kind man gave us this fine turkey. And now look at how his generosity has multiplied. These are the ripples of kindness."

Peter took in the sight his father was showing him. There were easily a hundred people who came through the Cratchit's house that night, most enjoying their first taste of turkey. No one left hungry, and every soul thoroughly enjoyed eating, drinking, dancing, and singing during this merry Christmas, indeed.

The clock had long ago struck midnight by the time Robert and Emily made their way to bed. Robert smiled, thinking back to the turkey that had started the day's festivities. He was reminded of the innocence of Tim's suggestion: that Mr. Scrooge had somehow been the mysterious anonymous donor. *Hmmm*, he thought, *maybe Mr. Holloway, or even Mr. Knight. Could have been anyone, I suppose—anyone other than Ebenezer Scrooge, that is.*

Chapter 28

The morning after Christmas, Robert woke knowing he was late, remembering Scrooge's orders to be at work "all the earlier" this day. He grabbed his coat and scarf and ran the 16 blocks, faster than he had on his first day of work as a boy.

The ripples you create return to you in waves. That's what Father used to say, at least, Robert thought to himself, as he hurried through the bustling London streets, pondering whether or not his tardiness following a day of Christmas merriment would leave him unemployed and his family homeless.

While he ran, Robert thought also about the last twenty-four years since the day he'd stood before Scrooge and Marley as a trembling twelve-year-old boy, desperately trying anything he could to keep a roof over the heads of his mother and sister. Since that very moment, he had served Scrooge and Marley faithfully, enduring their harsh treatment.

Still, and more importantly, working for Scrooge and Marley had put him in the path of countless people who he had been blessed to serve. And in his service, he had been able to find so many others willing to help in their own way. *Yes,* Robert reminded himself, *I believe now, as I did before, it was worth it.*

For whatever reason, I am a better person for having been in the service of Mr. Scrooge and Mr. Marley.

Robert stepped into the office sheepishly, hoping Scrooge might not notice the time on the clock and therefore his lateness. Quietly slipping into his chair, he tried to take up the business of the day before Scrooge saw he had been gone at the time he'd agreed to be at work.

"Cratchit!" came the stern, all-too-familiar demanding voice from the inner office. As well as Robert had prepared himself for this encounter, he still felt the proverbial sickness in his stomach, while his heart raced in his chest.

Making his way to his place before Scrooge's desk, Robert waited to be addressed. Scrooge continued to write in his ledger, knowing his employee was standing before him, allowing the tension to build and giving Robert a few more moments to anticipate the consequences of his tardiness. "What do you mean, coming here this time of day, Mr. Cratchit?"

Robert quickly responded with his apology. "I am sorry, sir, I am behind my time. I was making rather merry yesterday, sir, and the morning crept up on me."

Scrooge looked up from his ledger and returned his quill to its holder next to the ink well. Robert watched, as the veins swelled and pulsed on Scrooge's high forehead, knowing he was building into a rage that would be painful both emotionally and physically. Robert's knees quivered, just as they had when he was a young lad, standing in this very spot, begging to work for the men who had sent his father to debtor's prison for failing to pay the rent.

"Well, I tell you, Mr. Cratchit. I am not going to put up with this sort of behavior from you anymore." Robert bowed his head, resolving to accept his fate, as Scrooge continued. "Therefore, Mr. Cratchit . . ." Scrooge stood to face his clerk eye-to-eye, stretching the moment of confrontation as long as possible. Pointing his bony index finger directly toward Robert's nose, he said ". . . I am going to raise your salary!"

Scrooge dropped back to his chair, relishing in the expression on his clerk's face. Knowing he had just pulled a devilishly clever prank, he regretted there was no one about to enjoy the scene as he did.

Robert raised his head to see Scrooge point toward him and laugh profusely. "Sir?" asked Robert, questioning whether he had heard his employer correctly. For Robert had never before seen Scrooge laugh like this. Occasionally, he'd suffered through the evil laughter of a man who had bettered another man in business, or cackled about a profit at the expense of someone else's misfortune. But this was quite different. Scrooge was holding his hands across his belly, as though he was unsure if laughing so hard might damage his stomach.

The confused look on Robert's face was just the expression for which Scrooge had hoped, and it was precious indeed. Unable to form a complete sentence through his own laughter, the best Scrooge could manage was to nod his head and blurt out an occasional "Yes!" Finally, Scrooge regained his composure and realized he best explain himself, as Robert was not laughing with him.

"Oh, Bob," Scrooge began, with a more composed demeanor, "I have not lost my senses. Indeed, I have found them. I *am* going to raise your salary, and help you care for that family of yours, if you will let me."

Robert stood in shock, unable to speak or move. His knees no longer trembled, as he felt all the tension leave his body. Still, he did not know what to make of the situation. Was he in another dream from which he would soon awaken? Had Scrooge lost control of his mind? *Perhaps,* he thought, *the old man fell or was kicked on the head walking too close to the back of a mule.*

Scrooge slapped his hands together and rubbed them, trying to produce some warmth. "Cold," he said with a shiver. Throwing a fist full of coins on his desk in front of Robert, he said enthusiastically, "Go out and buy us another coal scuttle! Yes, you do that before you dot another 'i' or cross another 't', Bob Cratchit!"

Robert reacted to the order without question, as twenty-four years of training had taught him. He gathered more than enough coins from the desk and darted for his hat and scarf. Before leaving, he stopped and turned to see Mr. Scrooge laughing like a drunken man at a street carnival. *That must be it,* Robert thought to himself. *He must be drunk, although I must say I have never known Mr. Scrooge to drink hard spirits in the past.*

Returning with a scuttle of coal, Robert immediately placed a single piece of coal in the embers of the stove, avoiding eye contact with Scrooge for fear he would be chastised for buying coal, or worse, for burning it. From behind Scrooge's desk came the voice he still barely recognized, "Stoke that fire, sir! Let's bring some warmth to this drafty hall!"

He looked in Scrooge's direction to see the man sitting behind his desk, hands clasped and still smiling just as brilliantly as when he had left the office minutes earlier. For the first time that day, Robert allowed himself to smile. He couldn't help himself, as Scrooge's laughter and smile were both absolutely contagious. Hearing Scrooge's words as more of a request than an order, Robert picked up the small coal shovel and slipped a shovel full into the stove.

Robert reached for a match to light the fire, but before he struck it, Scrooge called out, "Bob, wait!" After reaching for his walking stick, Scrooge unscrewed the silver ornamental grip, slid a finger deep inside the hollow compartment of the shaft, and retrieved a paper roll, which in turn he handed to Robert. "Here sir, use *this* to light the coal."

Robert unrolled the paper which read:

I, Robert Cratchit, do woefully and sorrowfully confess to the crime of stealing ten shillings from the business of Scrooge and Marley.

He looked back at his old employer—and, he could tell, new friend—with a deeply grateful smile before stuffing the paper beneath the coal and lighting the fire.

"That's better, isn't it, Bob? Now we'll enjoy the crisp December morn from the comfort of a warm and toasty office."

"Yes, sir, Mr. Scrooge. Yes, indeed." Suddenly, Robert found he rather enjoyed being in the presence of this delightful, mysteriously transformed soul. *Even if it lasts only a few more minutes*, he thought, *and the gruff old slave driver I've known him to be returns, this is a blessing to behold, indeed.*

As Robert walked back to his writing desk, Scrooge stood and walked toward him. Robert noticed that the man who normally walked with a stoop stood taller today, even leaving his cane standing in the corner. Reaching his arm around Robert's shoulder, Scrooge steered him away from his desk, toward the front door and said, "Plenty of time for work later, Bob. What say you to a piping hot bowl of mulled punch?"

"Yes, sir. Yes, that sounds like a fine idea!"

"Good, good!" Scrooge slapped Robert on the back twice, then suddenly stopped, as though he remembered something of importance. Robert stopped with him, as Scrooge turned quaintly serious. "Oh, and Bob," he said, taking Robert's hand in his. "Merry Christmas! And I mean a merrier Christmas than I have wished you in many a year, or *ever*, for that matter!"

Robert was still slightly stiff with the anticipation of some sort of retribution from the man who, until this very morning, had been a mean-spirited tyrant. With a smile and hearty handshake, though, Robert returned the gesture with his own joyous smile. "Thank you, Mr. Scrooge, and a very Merry Christmas to you, as well."

Scrooge held Robert's hand firmly, while looking directly into his eyes. Robert could not comprehend the transformation, but for the first time ever, he saw the light of a loving spirit there in Scrooge's face.

Before releasing hands, before stepping out to enjoy the crisp morning air and sharing a bowl of Yuletide punch, Scrooge expressed one last sentiment with heartfelt sincerity: "Your servant, Bob—your servant."

ABOUT THE AUTHOR

Dixie was born in Germany and later moved to the States with her family. She earned her certification as a Radiological Technologist in Lexington, Kentucky, and currently resides in Huntsville, Alabama with her husband and children. A mother of three and grandmother of three, she has proudly served her local church as a teacher for over thirty years. It was through her love for children and storytelling that she found her passion for writing fiction and reading the classics.

Made in the USA
Columbia, SC
25 September 2019